LIGHTS, ACTION, YOU!

The Guide to Master Your Mindset, Overcome Work
Stress, and Regain Your Personal Freedom

ROBERT A. LANE

You are the CEO of you!

Robert A Lane

Lights, Action, YOU!

The Guide to Master Your Mindset, Overcome Work Stress, and Regain Your Personal Freedom

Robert A. Lane

Cover Design by 100 Covers

Edited by Bethany Davis

All photos were taken by Robert A. Lane and are part of his personal collection.

For more information: support@rrpproducts.com

ISBN: 979-8-9869350-0-3

Contents

Freebies and Bonuses!

Use this link— bit.ly/3L02Z7Q-FreeBonuses —or scan the QR code below to get some awesome freebies, bonuses, and supplemental materials that will enhance your reading experience!

This book is dedicated to my colleague and friend Jason Risk, who unexpectedly left this earthly world right before this book was published. Without his support, inspiration, and crazy antics, some of the stories in this book wouldn't exist.

You are sorely missed.

Introduction

HOW TO GET THE BEST EXPERIENCE FROM THIS BOOK

I'm Robert A. Lane, and I am a corporate performance coach. I help busy professionals eliminate stress, overwhelm, and burnout so they can achieve true work-life balance, regain their personal freedom, and take their careers to the next level. Before I became a coach, I spent thirty-plus years working in various facets of the entertainment industry, and I understand firsthand what it's like to be on the corporate "front lines."

When I set out to write this book, the goal was to provide you with valuable tools and techniques to help you to not only be more productive, efficient, and stress-free at your job, but also to be able to apply these techniques to your personal life. You deserve to live your life at its highest level!

Lights, Action, YOU! is not your typical self-help and personal development book. I share some of my best stories from working in the industry to give you an inside scoop on the glamorous—and not so glamorous—parts of the entertainment world, then tie each story together with the tools and techniques I teach my clients in my coaching program, The Mindset Method.

Each chapter opens with a movie quote from some of my favorite films, hand-picked and specially curated to set the stage for the ensuing entertainment industry story and the valuable lessons taught regarding the topic for that chapter.

There are three basic concepts you need to understand to get the most out of this book:

- Mindset: No matter what your goals are, whether they are career, financial, relationship, or even weight-loss goals, you have to be in the proper frame of mind before you start your journey. Starting with the right mindset will lead to success.
- Implementation: There are a lot of great tools in this book, but you have to implement them in your life to reap the full benefits. Inaction equals stagnation, and that's not good.
- Consistency: It's important to be consistent with applying these tools and techniques. Consistency will create new habits that will lead to positive permanent lifestyle change. That is true transformation!

Now go and enjoy the stories, and take all the lessons learned to heart!

Don't forget to grab the free bonuses and supplemental materials that go along with the book!

Use this link: bit.ly/3L02Z7Q-FreeBonuses

Or scan this QR code:

Free Bonuses!

ONE

The "Eyes" Have It

Matt Hooper: "It doesn't make much sense for a guy who hates the water to live on an island either."

Chief Brody: "It's only an island if you look at it from the water."

Jaws

When I became inspired to write this book, I decided to take a mental journey back to the moment when I was first exposed to the entertainment world. I had to go way, way back to a time when I was just a little kid.

I grew up in a quiet suburb called Shadow Hills, a small area tucked away in the eastern part of the San Fernando Valley in Southern California. The neighbors who lived behind me were Robert and Charlotte Mattey and their grandson, Craig. Craig and I ended up becoming best friends. I think we first became friends when we were only three years old.

I spent a lot of time over at the Matteys' house. Craig and I got into plenty of mischief playing in his grandpa's workshop, a place we weren't supposed to play. One time Craig told me he had figured out what his grandpa was going to give him for his birthday. He said his grandpa was making him a train. I was thinking he was building Craig one of those Lionel train sets for kids. When Craig's birthday arrived, I was completely surprised to see that Mr. Mattey hadn't built a train *set*, he had built an actual motorized battery-powered train from scratch. It was huge, like a golf cart. The train was not only big enough for Craig to drive, but it could carry two more passengers! Mr. Mattey put these giant wheels on it so Craig could literally drive it around in the backyard. It was the coolest thing ever.

I didn't realize it at the time, but Craig's grandfather was the great special effects artist Robert A. Mattey. Mr. Mattey (as I always called him) had done the special effects for several Disney movies, including *Blackbeard's Ghost*, *Mary Poppins*, and *20,000 Leagues Under the Sea*. However, his biggest claim to fame ultimately didn't come from Disney. It came from Universal Pictures, and the movie was *Jaws*.

One day, while I was over at the Matteys', Mr. Mattey had received a phone call. He said Universal Pictures wanted him to come out of retirement because a director, some guy named Spielberg, had specifically asked for him to do the special effects for some movie about a shark. He grumbled about having to spend a few months on the East Coast to shoot the film, but he decided to take the job.

One day, Mr. Mattey asked Craig and me if we wanted to go see the shark he was building. We went with him to a big hangar and there it was, this giant shark. To us little kids, it was huge and scary. At the time, the front part was completed, but the back part of the shark was opened up so we could see all the mechanics and hydraulics inside. It was literally jaw-dropping! Mr. Mattey also showed us a couple of cages that he had built. I thought that they were shark cages, but I wasn't sure because the cages weren't much bigger than me or Craig. I think I was asking Craig if they were shark cages when Mr. Mattey said, "This is a shark cage. We're gonna put a midget in there to make the shark look bigger!" (Mr. Mattey always had a way with words. Political correctness wasn't his forte.)

I was utterly amazed that I was able to see how this giant mechanical shark was built. Looking back, there was no way any of us could have guessed how this shark would terrorize moviegoers for generations and completely change the movie industry. Mr. Mattey was working on the first-ever summer blockbuster.

I am forever grateful to Mr. Mattey for that rare opportunity to see movie magic created behind the scenes. If I had only thought to bring a camera. Back then, iPhones were nonexistent. We had Instamatics! They were the latest and greatest consumer camera technology at the time. Actually, I don't believe I owned a camera at all, but if I had . . .

A few years later, the Matteys decided to move to a quiet mountain town called Frazier Park. Craig asked me if I wanted the actual mechanical *Jaws* eyes from the original shark. Are you kidding?! Of course! He sold the eyes and a couple of shark fins (not used in the movie *Jaws*) to me for ten bucks, with explicit instructions, "Don't tell my grand-pa." We never discussed our business exchange again after that. He also asked me if I wanted the train that his grandpa had made for him on his birthday, and he was going to give it to me for free. I really wanted it, but my parents wouldn't let me keep it. I bet that train could have ended up in a special effects museum somewhere.

Craig driving the train with me at the caboose.

Craig didn't move with his grandparents. He ended up living with his father and stepmother and her two daugh-ters. I saw Craig many years later when I had a house-warming party. Honestly, I was surprised that I was able to track him down. It was great to see him again. Of course, I had the eyes and fins proudly displayed. Craig mentioned that he had an original script signed by everyone from *Jaws*, including the full cast, crew, and Spielberg himself. What a fantastic piece of movie memorabilia! I would love to have that script. That would totally complete my little *Jaws* memorabilia collection.

To this day, I still have the eyes and fins. I also have an article from a local Shadow Hills newspaper that did an in-depth interview with Mr. Mattey about the making of *Jaws* after the movie was released. There's a great picture that was published in the article where Mr. Mattey is holding one of the mechanical eyes. The other eye is lying on the ground behind him. You can 100% tell that the eyes in the picture are the same eyes I have, which is proof that they are the same mechanical eyes used in the movie and validates their authenticity. At one point, I joined a private Facebook group for *Jaws* fans called Jaws Finatics, where I shared my story and posted pictures. Joe Alves, the production designer on the movie, saw my post and also verified that these were the authentic eyes from the shark. Now, I don't personally need any validation because I was there and lived it, but for the naysayers, there you go!

I could sell those eyes for a lot of money. They are a rare piece of movie history. However, I hung onto them all these years because there is so much sentimental value attached to them. Will I ever sell them? I'd have to be really hard up for cash before even considering selling those eyes. I did think about the possibility of having them displayed at The Academy Museum of Motion Pictures if they are interested.

Article from the local paper about Robert A.
Mattey.

Original Jaws eyes.

There are a lot of great quotes from *Jaws*. I didn't want to use the go-to—"You're gonna need a bigger boat."—because it's overused and really doesn't relate to my story.

The reason why I picked the opening quote I did for this chapter is because it's all about perspective. Matt Hooper makes the comment to Chief Brody that it doesn't make sense for someone who hates the water to live on an island. Brody's response is actually brilliant: "It's only an island if you look at it from the water." Hooper tells Brody "That doesn't make sense," but I disagree. Again, it's all about perspective.

Perspective is the first of what I call the three p's: perspective, passion, and purpose. To deal with his fear of water, Chief Brody adjusted how he viewed his surroundings to ease his anxiety. Perspective is not based on your circumstances but on how you view them. In regards to your career, do you approach your job with positivity or negativity? Do you look forward to the next workday and wake up in the morning excited, or do you dread going to work and wake up with anxiety? Your perception not only sets the tone for your workday, but it also affects your mood. Every day, you have the opportunity to choose how you perceive your career—or your life, for that matter. If you decide to choose positivity over negativity, your perspective will ignite your passion, the second p.

Passion should be in alignment with perspective. For example, the *Jaws* experience began my fascination with moviemaking, which eventually led to a career in the entertainment industry. Seeing that shark being built gave me a new perspective on filmmaking, and it ignited a passion for the industry. That passion stuck with me my entire life. So many people go to college or trade school or do whatever it takes to learn a craft and land the jobs of their dreams. But, as time goes by, many fall into a routine and trigger work "autopilot." They forget how it felt when they got their dream jobs in the first place. Are you still passionate about your career? If not, go back to when you landed your first job. It didn't matter if it was entry level or even an internship. You got your foot in the door! How did it feel? Tap into that feeling because that's your passion. This leads to the third *p*—purpose.

Purpose is living with conviction. It's about being aware and embracing opportunities. Having purpose keeps you focused and gives you a sense of direction. Having purpose in your career means doing work that satisfies your passion. It allows you to be excited and to want to go to work each day, and it means more than just bringing home a paycheck. When the three *p*'s—again, perspective, passion, and purpose—are in alignment, you will be positively motivated to push yourself forward to reach your goals.

Even as a kid, after I saw the shark being built and then, soon after, went on The Studio Tour at Universal Studios for the first time, my three *p*'s were firing on all cylinders! I came up with this crazy idea to create my own "Universal Studios tour" in my backyard. I charged the kids in the neighborhood a nickel. I pulled them around my backyard in a wagon and had these cheesy movie experiences like the *Old Faithful* geyser and an "unexpected" landslide. A couple of friends helped me with the "special effects." After the tour, I would do a stunt show, riding my bike off a makeshift ramp and purposely crashing. It was well worth the nickel!

At first, I wanted to be a stuntman, but after I learned how to play guitar, I wanted to be a rock star. Finally, when I grew up, went to college, and graduated with a degree in broadcasting, I ended up landing my first job in the entertainment industry as an audio engineer for a radio station. My career took me to other facets of the industry with jobs in cable television, audio post production, and even acting. I scored music for several films and television shows and finally worked on the corporate side of the business as a scheduling manager for a big post house, which led to a project management position at 20th Century Fox. But the thing that tied all those jobs together were the three *p*'s. They all were part of capturing the magic of the entertainment industry that I felt when I first saw Mr. Mattey's work.

Even after I left Fox and became a corporate performance coach, my focus was still on helping people who work in the industry deal with stress and burnout. Working in the business gave me a ton of experience dealing with a variety of stressful situations. Now, as a coach, I've taken my experiences and the knowledge I've gained to help not only entertainment industry professionals but *any* busy professionals to live healthier, more balanced lives without feeling stressed and overwhelmed.

How do you perceive your job? Are you just as passionate as you were when you started, or has that passion faded? Did you give up on your passion and are you just working at a job to pay the bills? Have you lost your perspective and life purpose? Give some serious thought to where you are now, where you want to be, and the gap keeping you from reaching your goals. The three *p*'s will change throughout your lifetime, and you will need to reassess and make any necessary adjustments to accommodate. But as long as you keep them aligned, you will be successful.

TWO

Grats & Brags Are Better than Bacon

Bonnie Grape: "You're my knight in shimmering armor."

What's Eating Gilbert Grape

I love bacon. So do the Simpsons, especially Homer. I had the pleasure of being invited to my first big Simpsons party one year when my department did a lot of work for *The Simpsons*. Each year, *The Simpsons* team would hold a huge event on the day the "Treehouse of Horror" episode aired. This party was mind-blowing, complete with celebrities, great entertainment, and, of course, bacon—lots of bacon. When it was time for the episode to air, the party would come to a halt and we would watch the broadcast live. This first party that I attended was held in a couple of hangars at the Santa Monica airport. It was nothing less than spectacular. There were plenty of celebrities wandering around.

The date I brought to the party even danced with Gary Busey. I was lucky enough to grab a quick dance with Lisa Simpson.

The best thing about the event was the food. They had this incredible spread of almost anything you could think of. Did I mention bacon?? The dessert section was off the charts and it included a wonderfully unique delicacy: chocolate-covered bacon! (See . . . bacon does go with everything.)

The staff who worked for *The Simpsons* always kept our department on the invite list for future parties. This was a great perk, and I'm glad my department was able to do the number of post-production jobs that we did for them. In the building where I worked on the Fox lot, the *Simpsons* cast recorded their voice-overs every week. I was fortunate to have the opportunity to meet them. Another great perk was being allowed to feast on the food in the green room after the *Simpsons* sessions. It was a great way to make sure the leftover food was never wasted, plus I have a feeling it may have contributed to all of us gaining a few pounds. I'm forever grateful to have had such good friends at *The Simpsons* and for their kindness, friendship, and generosity.

There were two other events that Fox hosted for their employees. One was a barbeque and screening to celebrate the release of their summer blockbuster each year, and the other was their Christmas party. Again, nothing short of legendary. It was nice to feel appreciated by the studio, and I was very grateful to attend these events.

The entertainment industry is very unique. If you work in entertainment, you are in a business that most people can only dream of experiencing. Granted, this is true for most specialized industries, but there is an aspect of glamour that no other industry can match.

No matter what industry you work in, there are opportunities to feel special or exclusive. Whether you work for a big company like Google or Microsoft or a small boutique business, feeling grateful and proud of the work you do is commendable.

However, there is a dark side that I have seen impact some people. I will use the entertainment industry as an example since I spent so many years in the business, but this situation exists everywhere as well. Again, there is nothing wrong with feeling proud or excited about the industry you work in, but the danger is when you allow it to go to your head. This is where you need to be careful and keep your ego in check. In some extreme cases, people act like their jobs give them permission to treat others around them like second-class citizens. They drink the self-entitlement Kool-Aid. The sad part about not keeping their egos in check is how ego spills over into their personal lives. I have witnessed a really skewed mindset that goes something like this: "I can do whatever I want and break whatever rules I want to fit my own personal agenda. But don't you dare do that to me!" It's a very twisted, selfish lifestyle that has zero room for true gratitude and appreciation. It is important to be aware of your thoughts and beliefs because they drive your subconscious and ultimately, this is a destructive habit that can potentially hurt your career and personal life. To be clear, this warped mindset is not exclusive to the entertainment industry. It has permeated many careers or businesses and people have adopted it as their lifestyle. You need to purge this immediately.

No matter what your career is, ask yourself these questions. Are you truly grateful and appreciative for the job you have? Are you proud of what you do, and are you doing it for the right reasons? Do you operate with a sense of self-entitlement, or is your ego in check? Be truthful and honest with yourself.

Take a few minutes to stop what you are doing and mentally step outside of your world. Visualize being inside a transparent room and, as you open the door, you are able to leave your world. As you turn around to look back at this room, you see your life and the wonderful opportunities you have. Think about the things that you get to see or do that nobody else outside of the industry you work in can experience. Appreciate where you are in your life and fill yourself with gratitude. Create an affirmation, be specific, and start it with these words: "I am so happy and grateful . . ." For example, "I am so happy and grateful to work for [insert the company or industry you work for] as a [insert your job title]." Another example can relate to an accomplishment that you are proud of. "I am so happy and grateful I finished my project ahead of schedule." Repeat the affirmation until you genuinely *feel* it.

I remember reciting affirmations many times while working at 20th Century Fox. I would walk around the studio lot and say my affirmations until I could really feel the gratitude and appreciation for my job. No matter how crazy or stressful it was, I was grateful to work at Fox. I had the opportunity to see and do things that I would have never been able to if I worked in any other industry. Out-of-town friends who visited me at Fox were enamored and even giddy to be on the studio lot. When I gave them makeshift tours, they were wide-eyed with amazement. It was their perception of glamour that made me realize how fortunate I was to be in the thick of it. Again, step out of your world, look back, and be grateful for what you have.

Here is a great gratitude tool that I started using when I began my coaching business and have used ever since. Every morning when I wake up, I write down three things that I am grateful for, no matter how big or small. The key component is to start your gratitude with two simple but powerful words: "I am." You can say things like "I am grateful I woke up this morning," "I am grateful for my kids," "I am grateful for bacon and chocolate," or "I am grateful my car is working." Find three things to be grateful for and write them down. Make this a daily habit.

The second part of gratitude is writing down your "brags." At the end of the day, before you go to sleep, write down three accomplishments that you are proud of, things you can brag about. Again, it doesn't matter how big or small these accomplishments are. For example, "I am proud that I finished my project on time," "I am proud I didn't fall asleep at the staff meeting," "I am proud I spent an hour playing with my kids after work," or "I am proud I didn't let my annoying coworker push my buttons." The key phrase to start the affirmation with is "I am proud . . ."

Buy yourself a "grats & brags" journal. It can be a notebook, three-ring binder, Moleskine journal, anything you want. Let it be something that inspires you and makes you happy when you look at it. Every time you see this journal, you know it is filled with so many words of gratitude and so many things to be proud of. I highly recommend a physical journal that you actually write in with your own hand. Writing by hand makes for a more empowering affirmation than typing on the computer. Write those affirmations down! As hard as it is to admit, physically writing down affirmations on a daily basis creates such a positive emotional boost that it is better than bacon! It takes a *lot* for me to say that, but for good reason. (If you are a vegetarian, replace "bacon" with a food you absolutely love. You get the picture.)

I wrote down two different choices for movie quotes to open this chapter. One was Clint Eastwood's line from *Dirty Harry*: "You've gotta ask yourself one question: 'Do I feel lucky?' Well do ya, punk?" Feeling lucky to work in this industry is definitely something to be grateful for. However, I decided on the quote from *What's Eating Gilbert Grape*. It's such a deep, heartfelt line that the mom says to Gilbert. "You're my knight in shimmering armor." Even though Gilbert corrects her by saying it's "shining," she tells him, "No, shimmering. You shimmer, and you glow." The amount of love and gratitude she has for Gilbert is overflowing. She knew how much he sacrificed for her and the family. Her gratitude and appreciation went deep down to her core. This is exactly how you should feel when you say your affirmations. Say them until you feel them in your core. I can't stress that enough.

No matter what your job is or how high up you are on the corporate ladder, always be grateful and appreciate what you have. Always be proud of the accomplishments you achieve. We are all navigating through this journey of life, and we never know what's waiting for us around the corner. Each day is "gratitude day." Each day is "brag day." When you start and end each day with this mindset, you are ingraining an awesome positive habit into your subconscious that will benefit you for the rest of your life.

THREE

Blinders Are for Horses

Roy Batty: "All those moments will be lost in time, like tears in rain."

Blade Runner

I've been a Queen fan since I was a kid. Aside from the big hits and epic albums like *A Night at the Opera*, my favorite albums are their first two, *Queen* and *Queen II*. Both of these albums, especially *Queen II*, showcased how incredibly innovative and progressive the band was at that time and what an insanely creative songwriter Freddie was. Definitely worth checking out.

When it was announced that Fox was making a biopic about Queen and Freddie Mercury, that definitely piqued my interest. I was excited and looked forward to the movie's release. A week before the release date, Fox was holding a private screening and after-party on the studio lot across from the building where I worked. I remember it was on a Friday, and my work that day was exceptionally stressful. I was too busy to even think about the screening and after-party, in spite of my excitement. I was totally immersed in work autopilot.

Early in the afternoon, I began feeling overwhelmed. My project management work was normally high pressure, but this day happened to be more intense than usual. I needed to step away from my desk and take a break. As I left the building, I saw some guy walking towards me, and I looked up. He gave a little smile and continued to enter my building. As I walked away, I said to myself, "Probably someone famous . . ." and kept walking. The only thing on my mind was the amount of work that had to be completed that day, and I didn't even give a second thought to who had just walked past me.

The policy at the studio regarding celebrities is to not approach them. They are there to do a job, just like anyone else, and they are not to be disturbed. I've seen quite a few celebrities, and the most interaction I would have with most is to say "hello" and go about my merry way. Unless they struck up a conversation with me, I would respect them and not encroach on their personal space. Granted, there were some celebrities I was really excited to see, but I kept my cool and was always professional.

Later in the afternoon, the after-party was in full swing. They held it outside, between the screening theater and the building where I worked. I walked through the after-party, between all the people, as I was returning to my building. I saw the guy who had smiled at me earlier. I didn't think too much of it, as I was still mentally absorbed in the amount of work that I had to complete, and I was more focused on work frustration than on what was going on at the party.

I follow Queen's guitarist, Brian May, on Instagram. That following Monday morning, I was checking out his posts, and I saw a video he posted of himself riding in a golf cart on the Fox lot. In the video, he stopped right behind my building and got out to go to the screening. Then it hit me. The guy I had thought was "probably someone famous" was in fact Brian May! I had been so self-involved with my work and so focused on the pressures of the day that I had walked right by one of my guitar heroes without it even registering in my brain. And, to put more salt in the wound, when I had walked through the after-party, I had walked by Queen's drummer, Roger Taylor, and all of the actors from the movie. Maybe Adam Lambert was there. Who knows . . .

Had I been present and aware of my surroundings and taken off my work blinders, I never would have missed meeting Brian May. In regards to the studio policy about not approaching celebrities, I would have thrown that out the window! When I first saw him as I left my building, I totally would have approached him, stopped him, talked to him, and asked him to take a selfie with me! I have no doubt he would have done it, too. He is always known for treating his fans very well, and he definitely has a genuine love for them.

Going to work each day and performing the same tasks becomes routine, and we end up functioning on autopilot. As the day becomes more stressful, we tend to become oblivious to almost everything that is happening around us.

I call this phenomenon "putting on your work blinders." Just like a horse that has blinders on, we are only focused on what is directly in front of us. Remove the work blinders!

How do you do this? By being in the present moment and not allowing the day-to-day pressures of your job to control you. Even if you are operating on autopilot, you can still be present and aware of your surroundings.

It's okay to have a routine at work, but operating on autopilot has its pitfalls. When you are doing the same thing every day, you end up adopting the autopilot habit. Not only does this create work blinders, it also affects how you show up. For example, maybe you have weekly or daily meetings. Are you just going through the motions or are you present and in the now? How you present yourself at these meetings is a strong indicator of how you present yourself to your clients. Are you energetic and awake or lethargic, always looking to hide in the corner until the meeting is over? Upper management observes and takes note of your behaviors, and that will have a bearing on whether you are considered for a promotion or not. Your work blinders may create missed career opportunities later on.

A missed opportunity can result in additional physiological and psychological anxieties. If you miss an opportunity or get passed up for a promotion, the experience can elicit feelings of regret and rejection. It is extremely important to get through the emotional side of regret and move on. If this is not handled, it can lead to depression, low self-esteem, and an overall lack of focus. You can also experience physical effects like lack of sleep, loss of appetite, or constant headaches.

Here are a few key points to help you move forward through any regret you may encounter from a missed opportunity. Own it, learn from it, and then move on. Owning it is accepting the outcome. Learn the lesson from the situation. Was it your action or lack of action that contributed to the missed opportunity? Were you present and in the moment or on autopilot? Understand that the lesson is not punishment but growth. Once you learn and embrace the lesson, you can move on and leave regret behind.

Be forgiving of yourself. Acknowledge the choices that you made, don't beat yourself up about it, and accept that this is now in the past. Use the experience as an opportunity to change and grow, especially if the experience was a negative one. Again, a lesson equals growth and greater self-understanding. The key factor is being able to work through the emotions, not sit in them. It is very important for your physical and mental health to work through any challenges that come up, not wallow in them.

The line from *Blade Runner* is the last thing that replicant Roy Batty says right before he dies. It's not only his life experiences that will be lost "like tears in rain," but any chance he had of living longer to experience more life is lost as well. Although Roy was the antagonist, he did live his life to the fullest. He lived in the present. He lived in the "now." This is how you should live your life. Be present and in the "now." Take off those work blinders. Unlike Roy, you have your whole life ahead of you to take advantage of any opportunities that come your way. When they do, grab them!

FOUR

Ain't Talkin' 'Bout Brands

C.D.: "I said 'Ten more seconds and I'm leaving.'
Wait a minute. What'd you think I said?"

Roxanne: "I thought you said 'Earn more sessions
by sleeving.'"

Roxanne

Communication is a skill that takes practice to master.
Understanding the different components of good communication and how they work together will help you with
your career goals and personal life. Once in a while you
may run into a situation where normal communication is
not the norm. Better watch what you say!

A few years before I worked at Fox, I landed a radio gig at
Playboy Entertainment Group as an audio engineer for

their new radio show called *Night Calls*. This was actually a spin-off of the *Night Calls* TV show. Satellite radio was a new venture for Playboy. This was back when XM Radio was the only satellite radio service available, before Sirius. In addition to the normal subscription price for XM, Playboy Radio charged an additional three-dollar subscription fee. The reason for this was that they could say anything they wanted on the air. They could talk sex and swear up a storm without being regulated by the FCC or anyone else. Communication was wide open. There were no boundaries.

However, Playboy implemented an interesting policy for the show. No one on the air was allowed to say any brand names. This included names of products, companies, anything that was associated with a brand. So, if a caller was telling a story about how he had a dream he was having sex with Minnie Mouse at Disneyland on the It's A Small World ride, Playboy would freak out. They were afraid of offending another business and being sued.

Another responsibility I had as the audio engineer, aside from the usual technical duties, was to enforce another policy Playboy implemented, which was cutting off any callers who sounded like they were going to "get off" while on the air. If a caller sounded like they were having sex or about to orgasm, I would immediately cut the call off the air. Playboy's other fear was, again, being sued because some guy got in a car accident while jacking off listening to the show.

Finally, there was one more responsibility added to my engineering tasks. I had to keep a detailed log so whenever a brand name was mentioned on the air, I had to write down what was said, the time it was said, and who said it. We were live on the initial broadcast, so nothing was edited out, but when XM did replays of the show, they would go back and edit out all the brand names from the list that I created.

This may not seem like a big deal, but think about it. Every day, communication involves saying a brand name. "Can you grab me a Coke out of the fridge?" *Coke* is a brand name. The proper terminology is *soda* instead of *Coke*. Other examples would be saying *facial tissue* instead of *Kleenex*, *headache medicine* instead of *Tylenol*, or *cell phone* instead of *iPhone*.

Juli and Tiffany (the two cohosts of the show) and I turned this into a self-censoring game or competition. If one or the other said a brand name, they would call each other out. The winner of the day was the person who said the fewest brand names. When the competition started, it was hard for them not to say brand names, so my log ended up being several pages long each day. But, as time went on, Juli and Tiffany refined their communication skills. So, when one of them slipped up, it was a big deal, and they didn't hold back on letting each other know.

One day, Juli couldn't make the broadcast, so Tiffany was hosting solo. As she was talking to a caller, she mentioned that she had used to be a dancer on a show that aired on Fox. Once she said "Fox," I looked up at her, smiled, and wrote it down in my log. She stopped in her tracks and said to me, "What?! What did I say? 'Fox?' Are you kidding? You're going to get me for saying 'Fox'?" She flipped me off (in a loving way, of course) and said, "Fuck you, you . . .

radio narc!" From that day on, that became my character name on the show: Radio Narc.

Juli and Tiffany had radio names that were given to them by the listeners, which made a lot of sense. Since Playboy Radio was on XM, most of the listeners were truck drivers traveling back and forth across the country. When they called in, they didn't use their real names, they use their CB handles, things like Midnight Rider and Ace. I don't remember the names they gave Juli and Tiffany, but it was only fitting that mine became Radio Narc.

Cohosts Juli and Tiffany expressing their love.

Radio Narc baseball cap, a gift from a listener.

I worked at Playboy Radio for about a year and a half but was let go the day before Thanksgiving. The producer of the show had been informed by his boss about a week or so earlier and was kind enough to give me the heads up because his boss wasn't going to say anything to me until firing day. I was grateful the producer told me ahead of time, and I was sad that my Radio Narc days were coming to an end.

Not being allowed to say brand names is not a normal way to communicate, but it is a great example of being conscious and aware of what comes out of your mouth. Thinking before speaking will keep you out of trouble and prevent you from saying something you will regret later. Here are a few key points that will help you improve your communication skills.

Active listening is one of the most important skills you can have, yet it's often thrown to the wayside. How many times have you been in a conversation where the person you are talking to is champing at the bit to respond or even cuts you off mid-sentence to finish *your* thought for you? Or have you done this yourself? This is not listening. You are so absorbed in your own thoughts that you are not paying attention to what the other person is saying. It's rude and disrespectful. This also shows the other person you really aren't interested, and your body language gives it away. Pay attention, be engaged, and rephrase what the other person is saying if you need clarification.

Speaking of body language, another good listening tactic is nonverbal communication. Do you have eye contact with the person when you are speaking? What is your body positioning? Are you standing or sitting with arms crossed or open? Do you appear approachable and engaged or closed off? Eye contact and open body positioning project trust. This will visually show that you are truly listening and interested in what the other person has to say.

When you are communicating, make sure to be clear and concise. Vagueness leads to misunderstanding, confusion, or misinterpretation of your message. When you convey your thoughts clearly and confidently, people will listen more intently, be open to your message, and engage in the conversation.

One important piece of communication happens within your inner dialogue, and it's negative self-talk. Most of the time, you are not aware of it. Once in a while, it comes out verbally, but most of it stays in your subconscious. Negative self-talk is a limiting belief you have about yourself or your abilities. When you say things like "I'm not good enough," "I can't do that," "I'm too stupid," or "I'm not pretty," you are ingraining these limiting beliefs into your subconscious, and this affects the decisions you make. Even if you are saying these things jokingly, you are still feeding yourself with negativity. Lack of self-esteem and not believing in yourself cause the bulk of negative self-talk.

Get into the habit of changing your verbiage to positive affirmations like "I can" or "I am." For example, if you feel you are not good enough or you can't do something, ask yourself why. Maybe it's something you can learn to do and become good enough. "I can learn this skill." "I am good enough to do the job." By identifying the areas in your life you think negatively about, you can change your perspective to be more positive. This will create a new habit that serves you instead of holding you back. It takes time and practice to reprogram your thought processes, but it's not impossible.

The quote from *Roxanne* shows how easy it is to misinterpret things that have been said. Granted, in the context of the film, Roxanne and C.D. were in the middle of a heated argument, so that was a contributing factor to the misunderstanding. At least Roxanne followed up to get clarification on what C.D. said to her. Paying attention, actively listening, and being clear and concise will help you become a better communicator. And no more negative self-talk!

Make that promise to yourself before moving on to the next chapter.

FIVE

Is That a Quadricycle?

Stephen Hawking: "There should be no boundaries to human endeavor. We are all different.
However bad life may seem, there is always something you can do, and succeed at. While there's life,
there is hope."

The Theory of Everything

After my stint at Playboy Radio, I was having a hard time
finding a job that would bring in enough income to pay my
mortgage. It boiled down to a simple choice: stay in the
same situation I was in or sell my house. I looked at my
options and decided to sell my house and move into an
apartment. Now it was time to figure out my next career
move.

I still had a passion for audio recording and editing, so I decided to enroll in the audio engineering program at Los Angeles Recording School to hone my skills with the latest techniques and software, especially Pro Tools. Pro Tools was, and still is the industry standard when it comes to audio editing. Even though most of the program was music-based, they did have one class about the fundamentals of post-production audio in film. This was the class that grabbed my attention.

Doing my thing at Los Angeles Recording School.

LA Recording School had a job placement program, but the job leads they offered were either internships or entry-level jobs that paid a little more than minimum wage. I had made really good money at my previous jobs, so this was an eye-opener. Again, I was faced with a choice: start from scratch or keep trying to find higher-paying work somewhere else, even if that meant not working in entertainment. Even though I had a lot of experience, it was time to put my ego aside and build a new career path.

Through the leads on the LA Recording School job board, I found two jobs. The first was an unpaid internship at a small post house in Burbank. I took the job because it was audio post-production work using Pro Tools. I was a Foley Editor for a B horror movie, and this gave me the opportunity to really dial in my Pro Tools editing skills. The second job was working Sundays at a church as their live sound engineer. It didn't pay much, but it was a paying gig.

I ended up getting a third job at a full-service post-production facility in Hollywood called Post Logic Studios. I was hired as a runner, which paid ten dollars an hour. Basically, a runner does all the grunt work and menial tasks for the facility: cleaning editing bays, washing dishes, washing windows, making coffee and lattes for clients, vacuuming, you name it. Advancement was possible, but there was a "pay your dues" pattern you had to follow to make it work. You started out as a runner and did that for about one to two years. Then you were promoted to work in the tape and film vault, and that might last another year or two. While working as a runner or in the vault, you were expected to learn on your own time the skills of the trade you were interested in. For example, if I wanted to do audio post production, I would need to befriend one of the audio mixers and train with them as their apprentice. If you work with them long enough and do a great job, you may be hired as their assistant. The "pay your dues" process could take up to four years, or even longer.

One day, while I was washing dishes in the kitchen, the VP of the facility came down and struck up a conversation. Since I was one of the new "kids" and it was only my second week working there, he asked me "what my story was." I told him about my Playboy Radio gig and also how

I had done work for another cable radio station as their national director of affiliate sales and marketing. Three days later, the VP came down to the kitchen and offered me a position as the facility's scheduling manager. What a break! That meant that instead of working my way up the "pay your dues" ladder for four-plus years, I did it in two weeks! Granted, the job position was not in audio post production, but it was a legit corporate job in the entertainment industry, and that was perfectly fine. I quit the unpaid internship job but kept the live sound engineering gig I was doing on Sundays at the church along with this new scheduling management position.

I worked as the scheduling manager at Post Logic Studios for another two or three years until one day I received a random call from someone at 20th Century Fox. This person asked if I was interested in a project management position for their audio department. She went on to say that I was highly recommended but didn't tell me where the recommendation came from. For a second, I thought, "Is she really serious?" but then I was excited by the thought of working at a major studio. It was so strange to get this unexpected call, but it was a great opportunity. I told her I was definitely interested. I interviewed and got the job working on the studio lot at Fox, thus starting the next new chapter of my career. What had started as a low point in my career ended up being the highlight. I didn't allow worry, fear, or all those crazy thoughts that ran through my head to alter the decisions I made.

Here are some interesting stats. The mind processes around 60,000 thoughts per day. Most of these thoughts are ones you are not even aware of. 80% of those daily thoughts are negative. Of those negative thoughts, 95% are the same negative thoughts that you had the day before. Almost all of these are the things you worry about. Of all the things that you worry about, 85% never happen. The 15% that do happen either end up not being as bad as you thought or teaching you a valuable lesson through the experience. The fact is that almost all of your worries have no ground to stand on. They are based on your pessimistic perception.

Many people fixate on worries, especially ones that never come to pass, and replay them in their minds over and over. This is a bad habit, and you need to break the pattern. All the focus is on the worry and not on the potential solution. Do not allow worry to dictate your actions.

Fear-based worry could have destroyed my career. I had to make some tough choices, like selling my house and starting my career from scratch. I could have given up and settled for a job that was unfulfilling but paid the bills. When I got sick of that job, I would probably have moved on to another one and then another one and so on.

This type of behavior creates a vicious cycle, which keeps you feeling stuck, stagnant, and unaccomplished. However, there is a method of approach that can break this pattern. It's called the Cycle of Outcomes. There are four parts to the cycle: the event, the story, the feeling, and the action. I also refer to this as the "quadricycle," a catchy way for me to remember the four parts of the Cycle of Outcomes.

The first step in the cycle is the event. An event is something that occurs in your life. The event itself is neither positive nor negative. It is neutral. For example, when I was told that upper management at Playboy was going to lay me off the day before Thanksgiving, that was the event. Again, the actual event itself is neutral. Being laid off was a neutral fact. Once the event occurs, it leads to the second step in the Cycle of Outcomes.

The second step is the story you create around the event. The story is actually a belief you tell yourself. The story itself is still neutral. So, a story I would create around being laid off might be that I'm always struggling to make enough money. Again, the story you are telling yourself is neither positive nor negative. Once the event happens and you create the story, it generates a feeling, which is the third step of the cycle.

Now come the feels. The event is neutral, and the story you created from that event is also neutral, but the feelings you associate with the story are positive or negative. Going back to the example, let's go through the cycle. The event was that I was being laid off. The story or belief I told myself was that I would always be struggling to make enough money. The feelings associated with my story were anger, worry, fear, and frustration. All the feelings come out in this step of the cycle.

The final step in the cycle is action. Your action is based on the feelings generated from the story. This last step can either be an action or inaction. My action from the feelings I had about being laid off could have been taking any job, even if it didn't pay well, because I had resigned myself to believing my story that I would always struggle to make more money. Or my action could have been inaction, not doing anything but instead selling the house and moving back in with my parents. Your action then takes you back to the beginning of the cycle, and the loop begins.

Once you are back at the top of the Cycle of Outcomes, this can easily lead into another negative cycle. You are now developing a pattern or bad habit. The beauty of the Cycle of Outcomes is that the negative pattern can be broken. Two of the four cycles—the story and the action—can be changed or altered to yield positive results.

So, using my example, the event was that I was laid off. To begin breaking the negative pattern, I first changed the story. Instead of telling myself that I would never be able to make enough money, I told myself that money was not a problem because I would sell my house. This new story created different feelings. Some feelings of disappointment may have remained, but instead of anger, I felt determination. The feeling of determination then changed the action step. My action step was putting the house on the market and continuing to find a solution that would allow me to still work in the entertainment industry that I loved.

Change your story or change your action. These are two steps in the cycle that you have full control over. You will either break a bad pattern or, better yet, stop a bad pattern from being created in the first place. Again, bad patterns are actually bad habits that do not serve you. Create new habits that do serve you and get rid of those bad ones.

Most importantly, stop creating scenarios of worry. Worrying about things that have not come to pass is a waste of energy. And again, if something you are worried about happens, usually there is a lesson to be learned. Embrace the lesson, learn from it, and move on.

My favorite part of the quote from *The Theory of Everything* is "there is always something you can do, and succeed at." The way the events played out after Playboy Radio is a perfect example. There is always something you can do. If you don't allow your worries and fears to take over, you will succeed. Understanding the Cycle of Outcomes and using it will guide you to better decision-making. The stories or beliefs you create will be much more positive.

If you would like a great one-sheeter about the Cycle of Outcomes, make sure you grab your free bonus materials if you haven't already. You'll find this one-sheeter—"Chapter 5—Cycle of Outcomes"—along with all the other bonuses for the book on the free bonuses page. This freebie is a great reference tool and a reminder that you can control the cycle.

Here's the link again— bit.ly/3L02Z7Q-FreeBonuses —or you can scan the QR code at the end of the chapter.

Free Bonuses!

SIX

Everyone Can Be a Manager . . . of Time

Troi: "Timeline? There is no time to talk about time! We don't have the time! . . . What was I saying?"

Star Trek: First Contact

Time is an interesting concept. Before I started writing this chapter, I was thinking about *Back to the Future* or *The Time Machine* or even Einstein (the physicist, not Doc's dog). The manipulation of time . . . We all have our share of "what ifs" and "if onlys." I know I do, and sometimes I wish I could go back in time and change circumstances or do things I didn't do or stop myself before I did things I did do. However, I know that if I were to actually go back and make those changes, they would cause a ripple effect, and my life would be completely different from what it is now.

The real "if only" is "if only I were able to see what would happen or what the end result would be if I changed something from the past." Wouldn't it be great to see the outcomes of each different decision and line them up side by side, then pick the best outcome and choose that to be my life? It sounds great on the surface, but then that would take away the excitement of the unknown, and it would definitely take away all opportunities to learn and grow as a person.

We need to embrace the time that we have. Let's start with one simple fact: we all have the same twenty-four hours in a day. So how come some people are much more successful than others? What is the secret sauce successful people use that unsuccessful people don't? Time management is a skill, and once you master it, you can live life on your terms, both at work and in your personal life.

When I was put in charge of encoding over 1,300 Fox features for the Movies Anywhere project, the cloud-based streaming platform, time management was crucial. I was given a short window of time to complete this assignment. The project was such a huge undertaking that upper management did the unthinkable: they actually hired a temp to assist me. We were always asking for help because the workload was insane, but usually we were turned down each time, so this was a big win.

On top of overseeing this project, I still had to deal with answering over 300 emails daily, in addition to handling regular meetings and phone calls. When all was said and done, we completed the project ahead of schedule. We also provided almost three times as much content to Movies

Anywhere than any other major studio in town. I found out afterward that the supposed deadline was a department deadline, not a deadline set by the client. We were busting our asses to stroke upper management's ego. But I wasn't too upset about that because I had accomplished a monumental task, and that was something to be proud of. The bottom line is that this would not have been possible if I hadn't implemented some serious time-management techniques.

What do you do with the twenty-four hours you have in a day? Give this some serious thought because how you utilize your time will make all the difference between success, stagnation, and failure.

The first thing you should do is a time audit. You need to see exactly how you spend your time on a typical day. Grab yourself a notebook and do the time audit for two to three days. Create a log and write down everything you do for one full twenty-four-hour day. You can start it at any time, but make sure to keep track for the full twenty-four hours. For example, if you wake up at 6:00 a.m., start your time audit and track everything you do until 6:00 a.m. the following morning.

If the first thing you do when you wake up is check social media, keep track of how much time you spend doing so. Then track exactly how much time it takes you to shower, get dressed, eat breakfast, drive to work, work, take your lunch break and rest breaks, drive back home, cook dinner, eat dinner, watch TV, get ready for bed, and even sleep. Track everything and the exact amount of time spent doing it. If you don't have a notebook, you can use an online calendar. Just make sure it is immediately accessible so that you can accurately log your time. Then repeat this procedure for one to two more days.

Once you are done with the time audit, review the data. You now have a record of exactly what you do and how much time you spend doing it. You will discover patterns and also see what tasks you do that take up the most time. Some of these tasks are a real time suck (maybe you didn't realize how much you watch TV or spend time on social media). You will also see where you can be more productive and efficient at work, or notice that you do have time to work out or spend more quality time with your family.

Another time-management technique is eliminating distractions. The time audit will show you everything distracting you from the job at hand. Your brain is a super computer. Just like any other computer, it focuses on one thing at a time. What you think is multitasking is actually not. The tasks done by a computer are done at a blistering speed that creates the illusion of multitasking.

The truth is that multitasking has been scientifically proven to be a lie. You are never working on multiple tasks at the same time. In reality, you are switching from one task to another and then back and forth, which is highly inefficient. When switching from one task to another, you never allow your brain to achieve a deep work state, immersing yourself in total uninterrupted focus. Deep work allows you to produce the highest quality work with the fewest mistakes. Multitasking is a distraction. Interruptions are distractions. Eliminate all distractions when you need to do deep work. Turn off your phone. Ask to not be disturbed. Stay focused on one task at a time, and your productivity will skyrocket.

A third time-management technique is to set boundaries. This includes allocating specific times to do specific tasks. Block out time to check emails, work on specific projects, take breaks, hold or attend meetings, etc. Do not allow anyone—especially yourself—to violate these time boundaries. You must honor them.

A fourth tool for time management is creating to-do lists. There's a right way and a wrong way to create a to-do list. When you make a to-do list, how long of a list do you make? I used to start each day making my list of things to do. My list each day was supposed to be short. However, it never failed that my to-do list ended up being twenty to thirty tasks that I thought I could complete. As I looked at the list, I knew there was no way I was going to complete it. Also, just looking at it made me stressed and overwhelmed.

Instead of making huge lists every day that you end up never completing, implement a technique called the Rule of Five. Before you go to bed, think of the five most important things you need to accomplish for the following day (no more than five!) and write them down. Be aware of which tasks move you forward and which ones do not. Many people do things that keep them busy, but it's just busy work. It doesn't move them forward toward their goals. In contrast, when you create this list the night before, your subconscious will already be thinking about how to complete the list while you sleep, so when you wake up you will be ready to tackle your day. Make sure to take into account realistic expectations for each task.

Once you have your list of five tasks, pick the one that is the hardest and highlight it. This is the first task you will do. I call the hardest task my "Ugly Ogre." Complete the Ugly

Ogre first, no matter how long it takes or how hard it may be. Once this task is completed, then go ahead and finish the other four tasks on your list.

When you complete the hardest task first, it makes the rest of your day so much easier and more productive. Getting the Ugly Ogre out of the way is a huge weight off your shoulders. You will find that the other tasks are easier to complete, and you may still have time in your day to add a couple more tasks. Your goal is not to carry over the Ugly Ogre to the next day. That's one of the biggest mistakes people make. Just get it done and off your plate!

Sometimes the Ugly Ogre can take the entire day to complete and you may not get to the other four tasks. Again, completing the Ugly Ogre is your number one priority. If this was the only task you completed for the day, great! Reevaluate the four remaining tasks, and if they are still essential to moving you forward toward your goals, include them on your Rule of Five to-do list for the following day.

By limiting the number of tasks on your to-do list and getting the hardest one completed first, you will actually get more things accomplished. It boils down to a combination of time management, workload management, and efficiency. The Rule of Five is a great technique to apply at work and in your personal life.

The quote from *Star Trek: First Contact* is great and definitely appropriate for this chapter. It sounds so convoluted and mixed-up. What a perfect representation of how most of us think! The fact is that we do have time. It's only a matter of managing it properly. You just need to take a quick moment to gather your thoughts and go from convoluted to clarity.

Remember, we all have the same twenty-four hours in a day. The people who are successful know how to manage their time and their workloads. They reach their goals and end up having more free time for themselves. There's no reason why you can't reach your goals and have more freedom. Implement these time-management techniques and you will be more efficient, plus you will reduce the levels of stress and anxiety you may encounter throughout your day. You will feel positive, energized, and focused. Once you master these techniques, you'll realize that you've found the secret sauce of success!

SEVEN

Help! I Need Somebody

Princess Leia: "Help me Obi-Wan Kenobi. You're my only hope."

Star Wars: Episode IV—A New Hope

As kids, we pretended all the time. It was fun playing characters like cowboys or monsters or superheroes. We could be anything we wanted. Making movies is the adult version of pretend. I've always wanted to make a movie, and in 2011, I finally had the opportunity to "pretend" as an adult when I made my first short film, called *I-DOLL*. I created a psychological thriller involving porcelain dolls . . . lots of them.

My uncle was a hoarder. He would go to thrift stores and buy things that he thought would be worth a lot of money later on. Most of what he bought was junk. My aunt, his wife, loved dolls, and she had a huge collection of porcelain ones. She wasn't a hoarder like my uncle. However, her doll collection was quite large. There were hundreds of dolls, many of them never taken out of their boxes.

When my uncle passed away in 2009, my aunt never went back to her house. She stayed with my parents and then eventually ended up in assisted living facilities. My aunt and uncle didn't have any kids, so there was no immediate family to take care of it, which meant the house was unoccupied.

Even though I had recently bought a house in Sedona, Arizona, I offered to stay at my aunt and uncle's house to be the caretaker of their property and help clean out the massive mess inside. I was still working at Fox, so most of my time was spent in LA anyway.

The house was packed. We're talking about a four-bedroom house with a huge family room and a separate building in the backyard, all filled to the ceiling with junk. And when you first walked into the house, you were greeted by sixty-five porcelain dolls standing in the living room. Some of these dolls were two or three feet tall. Most people would have been freaked out to see these lifelike dolls. However, it didn't bother me. What did bother me was the clutter, and I wanted to move the dolls out of the living room to make the space more livable.

Eventually, I was able to clean out one of the back bedrooms, and I decided to make that the "doll room." When I was done, I stood in the middle of the room and looked around. It was wall-to-wall dolls. Seeing those dolls staring at me from all directions finally freaked me out.

"Fuck this . . ." were the words that came out of my mouth as I left the room and shut the door.

The next day at work, I was telling my coworker Jason about cleaning out the back bedroom and moving all the dolls. I had already filled him in on the house situation, so he knew about my uncle's hoarding and the arduous task of cleaning the house that I had taken on. I told him how I was never freaked out about the dolls until they were all in the doll room. I said, "After I looked around and saw them all staring at me, I had to get out of there. So I left the room, shut the door—"

"You shut the door?!" Jason cut me off. He looked very serious.

"Yeah, I shut the door."

Then Jason said with a deadpan expression, "They're not gonna like that . . ."

I paused for a second . . . "Oh shit!" Needless to say, when I came home from work, I opened the bedroom door, apologized to the ladies, and never shut the door on them again.

Jason had suggested that I should write a movie or make a short film using the dolls. I gave it some thought, and, a few months later, in October 2010, I came up with the storyline. The script was written in literally one weekend. Pretty bizarre how it all flowed out, but sometimes the creative process works that way. Once I had a script, I needed to figure out how to shoot the movie properly.

Me and the ladies hanging out in the doll room.

I've had a lot of experience working on films in front of the camera and behind the scenes. I also did a ton of extra work. I learned a lot from observation, but not enough to put all the pieces together the right way. This first attempt at filmmaking had to be great. My biggest fear was that my film would be written off as a "student film" just because it was my first film. There's an unwritten expectation that the video, audio, acting, or all three is really going to suck for first films, and I wanted to crush this expectation no matter what it took.

It was time for me to seek help. I wanted to talk to people who had done this before and done it well. Luckily, I knew a lot of people at Fox, so the studio was a great resource. I talked to my friend Keith, who was a bigshot at Fox Search-light Films. He explained in detail the process of pre-production and gave me a ton of paperwork to use as reference material—logs, shooting schedules, shot planning guides, budgeting sheets, SAG actor agreements, you name it. He told me how much time I should spend planning before the actual shoot days and also shared some of his personal experiences.

I spent about two months in pre-production, and during that time I put together a great skeleton crew for the shoot. I held auditions and finalized my cast, did my location scouting, and built the sets for the movie. Everything was coming together, and by the end of January, I was finally ready to shoot.

The movie was shot in four weekends with an extra weekend for pickup shots. I planned each shooting day to make sure that I not only got all the scenes shot for that day but gave the actors plenty of space to do their best performances without being pressured for time.

It was supposed to rain on one of the shooting weekends, so that was a big concern. Luckily, I got help from someone who could handle weather better than I could, and miraculously, it rained in the neighboring towns but remained sunny where we were shooting. Got help from the Big Guy Upstairs, and He did it for free!

Most of the movie was shot at my aunt's house because that's where the dolls "lived." Plus, the house itself provided the perfect creepy vibe I needed. One thing I have to point out is that, after my uncle passed away, there were a few strange events that occurred at the house. Supernatural? Possibly. Specifically, my uncle's spirit? Maybe. It's been said that a person's energy remains in the possessions they owned, and considering how much my uncle hoarded, that would amount to a hell of a lot of residual energy!

I bring this up because, on the first day of shooting inside the house, there were a couple of weird things that happened. The first oddity occurred when I was taking behind-the-scenes photos during the shoot. One particular photo I took had this big orb in it. I immediately took a couple more pictures, but the orb was gone. Kennedy, the actress who starred in the movie, said she saw a face in the orb . . . and she was right, there *was* a face inside of the orb. Everyone saw it. I still can't explain where that orb came from.

The second weird event happened when we were shooting a scene in the kitchen. During the first take of the scene, as my character walked past a small desk in the entryway, a framed photo on the desk fell over backward. I heard the picture fall over, but I didn't see it fall. We were in the middle of shooting, and I didn't want to break character, so I played out the rest of the scene. Needless to say, the picture wasn't supposed to fall, so we reshot the scene. But here's the weird part. The picture frame itself has a locking stand. The only way that picture could have fallen backward is if the frame stand was manually unlocked first.

When I went back to watch the dailies the following week, I wondered if the falling picture was caught on camera. To my surprise and luck, it was! I decided to use that first take of the scene in the final cut of the movie and affectionately labeled it the "ghost take." Maybe my uncle had been messing with us during filming and he had knocked over the picture frame. He was always a practical joker when he was alive.

The last day of filming was the first weekend in March. The video portion of the movie was edited, and we had picture lock in April. It was time for me to tackle all the audio post production including sound design, music scoring, and the final re-recording mix. I needed a place to do a 5.1 surround mix. I asked the VP of my department at Fox if I could use the mixing bays in our building to work on the film on my own time. That was a big ask, but she said, "We're a movie studio. This is what we do. If you come in on your own time and you get permission from the audio department, then go for it." That was a big win! I received approval from the audio department manager, so I was good to go.

It was time to schedule the location and date for my movie premiere. I wanted to screen the movie in one of the big theaters on the Fox studio lot. That presented another challenge: renting a theater, any of them, would cost thousands. I wasn't sure if the person in charge of booking the theaters would give me a discount, let alone even let me use any of the theaters. I made sure I caught her in a good mood before asking. The plan worked, and she said I could book any of the theaters I wanted and we could work out the cost later. Even though I didn't know how much I would be charged, I went for it and booked my movie premiere on June 23rd.

The movie screening was a huge success. I was nervous as hell, especially since I had invited every bigwig I knew who worked at Fox. I received really great feedback. I was complimented on the "look." People enjoyed the music I composed. I was even complimented on my acting. But probably the best compliment I received was when someone said to me, "I will never be able to look at you the same way ever again." I love it because that told me I did my job creating this psychological thriller.

The official I-DOLL movie poster

By the way, the cost of renting the theater wasn't thousands of dollars. I was only charged $200, which covered the cost to hire the projectionist. That was another huge win, and again, I was very grateful.

I'm proud of *I-DOLL*. It may not be Academy Award material, but it did win Best Film at the Idaho Media Awards. It only took eight months to create, from conception to premiere, which would not have been possible without help from the people I reached out to who were better at certain aspects of moviemaking than I was. As much as it was uncomfortable and even risky, I still asked. I'm grateful to everyone who was part of the process: Keith from Fox Searchlight, who gave me all those production references, templates and pre-production advice. The VP of Fox Media Services, who allowed me to mix the film at the studio. Even the person who was in charge of all the theaters on the Fox lot, who gave me use of the theater for virtually nothing and only charged the cost of the projectionist. God even stepped up to the plate and provided clear weather for all my shooting days. But most of all, I have to acknowledge and thank my coworker Jason for planting the initial seed to create the film in the first place.

Finally, I have to give credit to my uncle's spirit for knocking over that picture frame and providing me with the "ghost take" that actually enhanced that scene in the movie. All these people provided something that I needed. All I had to do was ask. (Well, except my uncle. He unwittingly helped out without being asked, but I'm glad he did.)

If you need help, ask for it. If there are others around you who can do something better than you can, ask for their advice and guidance. Don't allow fear to stop you from forward progress. It's okay to show vulnerability. That's what makes us human. Asking for help from people who can do something better than you can demonstrates strength, initiative, and confidence. It shows you are not afraid to do what it takes to make anything you are doing the best it can possibly be. Plus, whoever you ask will feel honored that you sought their help or feedback.

One more important piece of advice. Don't wear too many hats. You can't do everything yourself and maintain the high level of quality that all those tasks need. I had a vision for *I-DOLL*, and I wanted to make sure I kept true to that vision, but trying to do everything was not the smart path to take. I was the writer, director, actor, composer, audio mixer, production designer, and more. It was way too much! I will never do that again.

They say that if you want something done right, you have to do it yourself. Not true. If you want something done right, put a team of people together who can do certain tasks better than you. Once you relinquish some of the responsibilities, the project will not only be completed properly, but it will exceed your wildest expectations! That shows confidence, accountability, and authenticity. Remember, asking for help exemplifies strength, not weakness.

EIGHT

Double-Bag It!

"I am who I am, I do what I do, and I am not ashamed of it."

Robert A. Lane

We all have our quirks. We all have funny habits and methods of doing things. When they are not the norm, people may look at you like either you're a clever genius, or you're outright stupid. Everyone has experienced some level of low self-esteem or lack of confidence. In the entertainment world, showing a lack of confidence can ruin your career—or so you think.

The truth is, thinking outside the box is allowing your creativity to shine. That's how new and innovative ideas are formed. But doubting yourself and seeking outside approval may hinder your creative outlet. So let me share with you a little story about thinking outside of the box . . . or bag.

I had a great gym bag. It was a double-bagged brown paper bag from Trader Joe's. I loved this gym bag. I organized it a certain way with my workout clothes, shoes, deodorant, hairbrush, and other gym essentials. It was perfect. There was a gym on the Fox lot, so that made working out very convenient. I went to the gym three or four times a week to do bootcamp classes or just work out on my own. The building I worked in was located on the other side of the lot from the gym, so it took roughly ten minutes to walk there.

My coworkers would tease me about my gym bag. They thought that it was ridiculous and asked why I didn't just buy a real gym bag. As far as I was concerned, my brown paper bag was my real gym bag. I told them it worked for me and laughed it off. Even in the locker room, other people would tease me about my gym bag. Again, I just laughed it off.

After a while, I started to become self-conscious and even a little embarrassed about my double-bagged brown paper gym bag. There were times when I felt anxious just walking across the studio lot. Finally, when I was feeling self-conscious about it, I took a moment and said to myself, "Who cares what other people think?" That's all I needed to say. I didn't say it in a mean or vindictive way. It was said as a statement of fact. "Who cares what other people think!" That's all I needed to do to give myself the confidence to continue my walk across the studio lot, go into the locker room, and do my workout or class. I would follow up that statement with this: "I am who I am, I do what I do, and I am not ashamed of it." Again, who cares what other people think.

As time went on, my coworkers would bring me brown paper bags and joke, "Look, I got you a new gym bag." I would respond, "Great! I'll take it!" Eventually, the people in the locker room who had used to tease me started saying that my brown paper gym bag was a pretty good idea. I told them, "Why should I pay $50 or $100 for a fancy gym bag when I can have one for free? When it wears out or gets too smelly, I toss it in the recycling bin and grab a couple of fresh bags. Saves me money and I'm not throwing out a plastic gym bag that can't be recycled."

My gym bag was quirky and definitely not the norm, but it served its purpose. I stuck to my guns and continued to use it no matter what other people thought. Nowadays, I do my workouts at home and go trail running quite a bit out here in Sedona, Arizona, so I don't have a need for my quirky gym bag. But if I decide to go to a gym again, that double-bagged brown paper bag will be back in action.

We allow ourselves to be influenced by others. This includes, friends, family, coworkers, shows we watch on TV or Netflix, and especially social media. If you allow external influences to guide your personal or emotional decisions, you are seeking outside approval that really has no bearing on your life. We have this innate desire to be loved and appreciated, so we are constantly seeking approval—but approval should come from within. Consciously, you may not even be aware, but your subconscious is. And since your subconscious drives the decisions that you make on a daily basis, you need to reinforce your self-worth to not only know but believe that you are worthy and great the way you are. It doesn't matter what other people think.

Here are a few things to keep in mind. Stop comparing yourself to others. Honestly, there is no comparison because you are unique. No one can ever be you, and that's what makes you awesome. Along with this is acceptance. In fact, don't just accept but *embrace* who you are. *Love* who you are. Don't second-guess yourself, especially if your doubt is being influenced by external sources. Trust your instincts. Finally, visualize successful outcomes instead of focusing on fear or embarrassment.

This is the only chapter that I didn't start with a movie quote. I felt my catchphrase warranted the honors because the affirmation itself holds a lot of weight. Plus, I couldn't think of a great movie quote about a double-bagged brown paper bag. If you come up with one, let me know.

So, the next time you go shopping, if the checker asks, "Paper or plastic?" go for the brown paper bag and ask them to double-bag it! Not only will you get an awesome gym bag, but every time you look at that brown paper bag, it will give you a little confidence boost as you say to yourself, "I am who I am, I do what I do, and I am not ashamed of it."

NINE

Fight, Flight . . . or Freeze

Ralphie: "It was all over. I was dead. What would it be? The guillotine? Hanging? The chair? The rack? The Chinese water torture? Hmmmph. Mere child's play compared to what surely awaited me."

A Christmas Story

After my experience of missing an opportunity to meet guitarist Brian May from Queen, I made a better effort to keep myself aware and present. Upper management was planning on creating a new encoding department at Fox. At that time, the digital file–based world was in its infancy, and Fox was on the cutting edge of developing and implementing this new medium. In fact, the department where I worked was instrumental in creating proprietary software and spearheading the digital file movement ahead of the other major studios.

The media services department I worked for took over the building across from where I was working to set up their encoding division. I didn't know much about encoding, let alone understand how the file-based world worked, but I saw this as a great opportunity to get in on the ground floor. I was currently working in the audio department, but I asked my boss about moving over to the new building and doing my project management work for encoding instead. I figured it was the best way to learn about this new medium, and I was excited to take on this state-of-the-art venture.

The first couple of days were really orientation days. My manager held a quick meeting to give an overview of the encoding world and then proceeded to list out a slew of operating procedures. Basically, we were taking movies and television shows archived on tape and transferring or encoding them into digital files. The perception I got from upper management was that we already had a solid grasp and understanding about encoding, but that wasn't necessarily the case. What made this even more difficult was that every few days we were given a completely new set of SOPs —standard operating procedures—that were vastly different each time.

As this was a really new world for me, I had a lot of questions and needed clarification, but I wasn't really sure what to ask. A coworker in the department seemed to understand it better than I did, but when I asked her a question, she blatantly refused to help. Her selfishness angered me, but that anger gave way to feelings of frustration and even a little bit of abandonment. I started feeling anxious and stressed about being able to perform proficiently in this new role.

It was time to get some answers. My manager came over to the building to check on us, and I started asking him questions. He immediately seemed annoyed, saying, "I already spent a half an hour explaining all that to you the other day," and walked away. My stress level shot up. I now saw that it was up to me to figure this out, so I dove into it the best that I could. There was no point in asking any more questions. I felt that that door had been slammed shut.

Work-order creation was a tedious process. It took a long time to put them together. However, time was working against me because tapes were piling in. There were so many stacked around my desk that I was literally buried in them. Again, SOPs continued to change every few days. Every time they did, the work we were currently doing had to be stopped down and new work orders created, meaning that we were basically starting from scratch again. As soon as I put one order in, I had four or five more features dropped off at my desk. The turnaround time kept decreasing, so my deadline window was shrinking each day.

There was no way to keep up the pace. The fear of never catching up became my new reality. The pressure was continually building and my anxiety level was off the charts. No matter how hard I worked to make this new venture successful, I felt I was failing. I wanted to prove to myself and to everyone else that I could figure things out. However, there were aspects of the encoding world I couldn't wrap my head around fast enough, and I felt I had nowhere to turn for help. I was afraid to ask any more questions, seeing how irritated my manager had been when I did inquire. I also didn't want to show any signs of weakness. Weakness meant admitting I was not capable. As a result, my stress and anxiety continued to climb to unimaginable heights.

It finally became so intense I hit "fight, flight, or freeze." Did I confront my manager and fight these never-ending procedural changes every few days, telling him he needed to offer help and guidance? Did I take flight and tell him I wanted to go back to the audio department, risking losing my job? Did I quit my job? No, I froze. I was just like a deer caught in the headlights. I decided the only solution was to stay at work as late as I could, accomplish as much as I could accomplish, and then go home frozen and defeated. All I had to look forward to was doing it all again, day after day. It was physically and mentally crushing me.

When all seemed hopeless, a little miracle happened. My manager came in and said that one of the project managers in our audio department was going on maternity leave and they would be short-staffed. He wanted me to cover for her until she came back. Relieved? Damn right I was! It took a lot of pressure and weight off my shoulders, and I was glad to be going back to a department I was familiar with already. It was also bittersweet, though, because I still felt like a failure. I had high hopes of getting in on the ground floor and being part of this new world. It just didn't worked out that way.

I went back to the audio department the following week, but the damage was already done. I had built up a lot of fear. My self-esteem was at an all-time low. The stress and anxiety I had created still lived inside me, and I felt the pressure of those emotions. I was still on edge, so when things became hectic, the fear and anxiety kicked in at a very high level and I was thrown back into fight, flight, or freeze mode. I lost my work mojo. I felt so beaten and fearful that one day I said to myself, "I can't do this anymore," and I went down to the VP's office, told her I was done, and actually had a nervous breakdown. I thought that this was the end of my career at Fox. However, my VP showed compassion and talked with me for a while to figure out what was going on and what I needed. She also set me up with some therapy sessions that Fox paid for.

I didn't have any tools to handle extremely stressful situations. Had I been taught such tools and techniques, the outcome would have been very different. As I went through the therapy sessions, I would tell myself, "The stress and anxiety *I* created . . ." That was an intentional statement. I realized I had a big part in creating my own stress from within. This led me to understand that not only external forces but internal forces can become stress triggers. You have to learn how to identify them.

So, what do you do? When you strip away the layers, stress comes down to one basic issue: fear. Most fears are based on false beliefs, but the physical and mental strains are real. When I created The Mindset Method coaching program, I developed a simple phrase that I use as a guideline to help identify fears and how to deal with them. Remember this phrase: "Face it, embrace it, purge it, replace it."

"Face it." This means acknowledging the fear, facing up to it no matter how dark it is. Stripping away the layers and exposing the root cause is the first step. Ask yourself what it is that you are really afraid of. Failure? Being fired? Divorce? Death? What is your deep-rooted fear?

"Embrace it." Now it's time to face this fear head-on. Again, this is about getting down to the root cause, which means asking yourself why you have this fear. Identifying the "why" is crucial. Talk about it out loud or journal it. Writing it down helps you to embrace your fear. I don't like using the term "confront" because that can cause fight-or-flight syndrome. You are not confronting fear, you are embracing it.

"Purge it." Once you identify the fear and understand the cause and why you have it, you can let it go. It sounds simple, but it is not as easy as it seems. Many people are resistant or outright refuse to let it go. Understand that when you purge your fear, you don't necessarily get rid of it forever. Instead, purging it allows you to work through it and come to terms with it. Then you can move it aside.

"Replace it." When you work through the fear and come to terms with it, you have made room in your subconscious to replace it with positive affirmations and gratitude. You shift your mind from a fear-based negative place of stress and anxiety to a positive place of gratitude, belief, and self-worth.

People do not want to show weakness. Most want to show that they are on top of their game. Let's be honest, most people would never admit that they didn't understand something, especially if it was essential or critical to their jobs. People also don't want to show fear because it is looked upon as weakness. But ignoring fear and not coming to terms with it can become debilitating, as it was for me.

The file-based encoding world was new and exciting. I wanted to get in on the ground floor of this new direction for the entertainment industry. My initial intentions were good. However, I allowed the fear of not understanding to get the best of me. Fear turned into lack of confidence, which triggered an insane amount of anxiety and over-whelm. This turned into fight, flight, or freeze. My lack of knowledge on how to handle fear and work through it led to my nervous breakdown.

Fear also clouded my perception. For example, the percep-tion of my manager being annoyed with me asking him questions could have been a reaction to the pressure and stress he was feeling from his own bosses to make sure the encoding department was successful. If I knew how to deal with my own fears, I would have been more present and aware.

The interesting aspect of fear is how easily it makes us go to a very dark place. That's why I picked the quote from *A Christmas Story* to open this chapter. In the movie, Ralphie said a very bad word in front of his dad, and he knew he was in deep trouble. Immediately, his fear took him to his dark place. He allowed his fear to get the best of him.

As much as I wanted to use my own catchphrase on how to deal with fear as the quote for this chapter, I felt it was more beneficial to present it as the lesson to be learned and the tool to put in your mental toolbox. This is definitely one phrase you want to keep with you at all times. "Face it, embrace it, purge it, replace it." It may save your sanity one day.

TEN

I Believe What I Believe . . . Believe Me!

Hashimoto: "Do you believe in ghosts?"

James: "I only believe in money."

Silk

Belief is an interesting concept. The basic definition of a belief is an acceptance that either a statement is true or that something exists. So, do you believe in ghosts? Do you believe in money? Do you believe in politics or religion? The fact is that beliefs are not real. They are only real to you. I'll dive into this later, but for now, I want to focus on one aspect of beliefs: believing in yourself.

Every year in the late spring, Fox held an event on the studio lot called LA Screenings. This was a very high-profile event where all the new TV show pilots were showcased to buyers, distributors, and studios from all over the world.

This was a very important event because it determined whether a new show was picked up or dropped. The shows that made it would premiere on the fall schedule. This was a very exciting time on the Fox lot.

Each year, my manager had the honor of choosing which project manager was going to be in charge of the work our department handled for LA Screenings. Having observed how intense the project was in the past, I was not going to volunteer. But, as fate would have it, this was the year I was chosen to be in charge. At that time, we were still using HD tapes as our video source. The file-based world was in its infancy, so studios were not integrating that format yet. Being in charge of creating all the content for LA Screenings was a high-pressure responsibility, and everything had to be perfect, even down to the labels on the screening tapes. I had to make a master tape of each pilot and then a backup master in case something went wrong with the first tape. There were multiple languages to deal with, as well as subtitling, captioning, formatting, and all sorts of details that, again, had to be perfect. The turnaround time from when we received the materials to when we needed to have all the assets created was less than twenty-four hours. Quite a bit of the work had to be completed overnight. Did I have enough belief in myself to confidently take on this project?

As much as I didn't want to be in charge, I took on the assignment and dove right in. I remembered how, the year before, the coworker who had been put in charge of LA Screenings would come to work around 5:30 a.m. or 6:00 a.m. and sometimes wouldn't leave work until after 2:00 a.m. He would go home and, four hours later, be back at work to do it all again. The LA Screenings project lasted for almost two months, and trying to function on twenty-hour workdays takes its toll. There had to be a better way, and I was determined to figure it out.

I developed a system to complete the daily tasks in a shorter amount of time. I segmented my days and made sure there was enough time allocated to solving any issues that arose. My workdays started at 6:00 a.m. I was able to complete all the tasks, prepare the overnight shift, and complete each workday by 8:00 p.m. Even with perfection being a requirement, I did not have to work until 2:00 a.m. like my coworker had the year before. I believed my system would work, and it proved successful. This was a huge confidence boost.

I had just finished shooting my film *I-DOLL* a couple of months before. I was in the post-production phase of going through all the dailies. I needed to go through them so that I could log which takes were usable. This applied to both video and audio. Some takes had great video but the audio was bad, and vice versa. I had a schedule to keep, so I was concerned about whether I would have the time to work on my film while handling LA Screenings. I decided that once I was done with LA Screenings for the day, I would set myself up in the back of the machine room and work on my film.

Since my system allowed me to finish my work by 8:00 p.m., I was able to spend another four hours on my film each night and go home at midnight. That still gave me enough time to rest and be fresh in the morning for another round of LA Screenings. I went from not believing I could handle the responsibility of LA Screenings to taking on two major projects at the same time.

I am happy to report that the LA Screenings project went off without a hitch. There were no issues, and the studio was very pleased with the work my department did. Upper management was also very satisfied, so that was icing on the cake. Even my coworker was impressed by how I was able to cut back on the number of work hours required and still get the job accomplished. All it took was believing in myself.

Beliefs are not real; they are only real to you. For example, let's go back to that earlier question: Do you believe in ghosts? There are people who believe in ghosts and others who do not. However, each person thinks their beliefs are real. So, in regard to the LA Screenings project, I believed that my system would save time and be more efficient, and that's why it worked for me. Another person could have looked at my system and not believed it would work. It was because I believed in it that it did.

Once you start believing that you are not capable of handling a situation or achieving a goal, you are buying into a false belief. You are telling your subconscious, "I can't." Those words are just as powerful as the words "I can." Why would you want to program your subconscious with beliefs that do not serve you?

Some of your beliefs were programmed a long time ago, and they have become very ingrained. However, you can reprogram your belief system to acknowledge any beliefs that do not serve you and remove them or replace them with beliefs that do. To do this, ask yourself a few questions.

What beliefs are holding you back? Had I not been assigned to the LA Screenings project, would I have volunteered? Not with the false belief I had. I did not have the confidence that I could successfully take on such a big project. The false belief was based on fear. This leads to the next question: How had this belief benefited me in the past? There's only one answer, and that is *comfort zone*. When something is challenging, the first reaction is to avoid being pulled out of your comfort zone. Excuses and procrastination are the go-to. If something is uncomfortable and risky, your subconscious will do whatever it can to remain comfortable. But if you give in, you are thwarting any opportunity for growth. Stepping out of the comfort zone is growth, and growth leads to success.

The next question I would ask myself is, "Can I think of a time when this belief was not true?" In the case of my belief about not having the confidence or skill, the answer was absolutely! I proved it to myself with the success of LA Screenings. Finally, I would ask myself, "What is it that I really want to be experiencing?" Confidence, success, and the belief that "I can." The most important aspect of this is experiencing the feeling. *Feel* confident. *Feel* successful. *Feel* what it's like to believe that you can! I definitely tapped into the feels after the LA Screenings project.

Make a list of your core beliefs and ask yourself these questions for each. By honestly answering each question, you will be able to determine if that core belief truly serves you or not. If it does not, then remove it and replace it with one that does. A core belief that serves you will move you forward towards growth, action, and positivity. Finally, come up with a few affirmations that will solidify your new set of beliefs. I replaced my false belief of not thinking I was capable of handling LA Screenings and replaced it with a new belief that I could handle it and be more efficient. My affirmations were statements like "I can excel at this project," "I am capable," "I am a leader," and "I can easily handle LA Screenings and work on my movie at the same time!"

The Asian horror movie *Silk* is one of my favorites. The movie is about a scientific team that captures a ghost and wants to find out who he is and how he became a ghost. The quote is from the opening scene, where Hashimoto, the head of the team, is hiring a Canadian photographer to take pictures in an abandoned apartment that is said to be haunted. Two beliefs are immediately established: Hashimoto believes in ghosts and James does not. James believes in cold hard cash, and Hashimoto cares more about capturing a ghost than he does about money. There are other subplots in the movie that also demonstrate beliefs from other characters. Each belief is real to the character who holds it, whether the belief proves to be right or wrong.

There was another movie quote I was considering for this chapter. It's from the movie *Miracle.* Coach Herb Brooks asks, "Who do you play for?" Mike Eruzione responds with the answer Brooks is looking for: "I play for the United States of America." Up to this point, each player had answered with their name and the college they played for individually, but Brooks was grooming the USA hockey team to become a *team* and stop thinking as individuals. Finally, he succeeded, and the USA hockey team collectively changed their belief system. As a result, they ended up winning the gold medal at the 1980 Winter Olympics. The odds had been stacked against them, and no one had thought that the USA hockey team had a chance. This pivot in thought created an "I can" belief that ended up accomplishing something that the world had thought was impossible. And, of course, this inspired the famous quote from Al Michaels as he broadcast the play-by-play in the final moments of the game when the USA team clinched the win over the Soviet Union team: "Do you believe in miracles?" The USA hockey team did.

Beliefs are not real, but they are real to you. Your beliefs and habits are what drive your subconscious. Feed your subconscious with positive beliefs and habits that serve you. Avoid any thoughts or beliefs that have any negative impact whatsoever. Being true to your core beliefs is important, but keep in mind that what you believe may not be what someone else believes, so be respectful.

If you would like a copy of my "8 Questions to Break Down Negative Beliefs," don't forget to grab your free bonuses for this book, if you haven't already. If you still need to, here's the link again: bit.ly/3L02Z7Q-FreeBonuses. (You can also scan the QR code at the end of the chapter.)

Crush those "I can'ts" and replace them with "I can." I believe you can do this!

Free Bonuses!

ELEVEN

The Verdict Is In

Sergeant Friday: "Just the facts, ma'am."

Dragnet

Let's have a little bit of fun. I've met a lot of celebrities throughout my career, including movie and television actors, athletes, and rock stars. There were quite a few that I had some sort of preconceived judgment or expectation about. Some of those preconceptions were positive, some were negative. My judgments were not necessarily accurate. In this chapter, I am going to focus on some of the best experiences I had with celebrities and whether my preconceived judgments were accurate or not.

I'll start with the first big celebrity I ran into (literally) when I started working at Fox. My office was located in one of the original soundstages on the Fox lot. On this particular day, it was time to clock out and go home. I grabbed my things and dashed down the stairs. At the bottom of the stairs, there was a side door to enter the building. As I got to the bottom of the stairs, the door opened, this man walked in, and I almost knocked him over. Luckily, I stopped myself just inches away from him. We both said "Whoa!" out loud. When I took a moment to get my bearings, I looked up and saw that I had almost knocked over George Clooney. My first thought was "Oh shit, I won't be working at Fox anymore . . ."

I apologized to him and he laughed about it. I told him, "Hey, it's the end of my workday and I guess I got a little bit excited." Again, he chuckled and said he understood. He was very pleasant and nice. I had heard or read in the trades about George Clooney having his moments, but I didn't sense whatever negative traits they had been talking about.

A smile says a lot about a person. In the same building where I had my George Clooney experience, I had another celebrity experience. Actually, this was a great building to work in because the scoring stage was on the first floor and the main ADR stages were upstairs on the floor where I worked, so I was able to see a lot of celebrities. On one of the busier days in this building, there were a lot of session musicians wandering around downstairs by the scoring stage. Most of these session musicians were older players. On this day I saw a younger guy walking towards me, and I looked at him thinking, "He's pretty young for a session guy." He looked at me and smiled. The smile gave it away. It was that unmistakable Tom Cruise smile. Tom saw me and said, "Hi, how's it going?"

That took me aback. I said, "I'm having a great day. How about yourself?" We had a little bit of banter between us, and we went our separate ways. I know Tom Cruise did crazy things like jump all over Oprah's couch when he was excited to be married to Katie Holmes, and a lot of people formulated judgments about him after that, but I found him to be incredibly nice. On the other hand, the people who worked for Tom left a lot to be desired. It's funny how the people who worked for him had the overblown egos, yet Tom Cruise himself was the nicest, most down-to-earth guy you could ever meet.

Let's change gears a bit and talk about rock stars. I remember when I was a little kid listening to *The Dr. Demento Show* on the radio. This one guy would send in cassette tapes of these goofy songs he wrote with his accordion that he recorded in the bathroom stalls at the college he was attending in San Luis Obispo. I remember when he sent in his first parody song, called "My Bologna," which made fun of The Knack's hit "My Sharona." It was Weird Al Yankovic. Dr. Demento gave him his big break. And the rest is history.

I had the pleasure of meeting Weird Al at the *Simpsons* "Treehouse of Horror" private party two years in a row. He was so nice and approachable and had no problem taking pictures with his fans. The second time I met him, I said, "Are you stalking me?" I told him how I kept running into him. He laughed about it and was happy to take another picture with me.

Speaking of *The Simpsons*, many of their episodes had guest celebrities. One of them was Lady Gaga. The studio made a big deal about her being on a *Simpsons* episode. The *Simp-*

sons actors recorded their voice-overs for the show in the building where I worked. On the day Lady Gaga arrived, most of the second floor was off-limits, including the green room and the building's kitchen. It was a bit overkill. Lady Gaga spent a good portion of her time in the green room. However, just after she arrived, she took it upon herself to go to the ADR stage and introduce herself and shake hands with all the staff. She was incredibly cordial and, if I remember correctly, took some pictures with the staff. A good friend of mine who helped run the recording sessions said that Lady Gaga told her, "I'm nervous." When asked why she would be nervous, Lady Gaga said, "Because it's *The Simpsons!*" Lady Gaga loved the show and was honored to be a guest on an actual episode. She wanted to do a great job, which she did.

When Lady Gaga was finished recording, she went downstairs to do publicity shots in her full-on rock-star persona. Here's the beautiful thing about Lady Gaga that makes her such an authentically genuine person. Upstairs, she was Lady Gaga, the down-to-earth courteous human being who was kind and respectful to everyone she met. Downstairs, for those publicity shots, she stepped into Lady Gaga the rock-star persona. She knew when to turn it on and off. That's what makes her a true professional.

Probably my absolute favorite celebrity I ever met was Robert Downey Jr. He was working upstairs in the same studio where *The Simpsons* cast record. He needed to record some voice-over parts for *The Voyage Of Doctor Dolittle*. It was lunchtime, and I went to the kitchen to microwave my leftovers. Robert Downey Jr. was sitting at the small kitchen table talking to a friend. Company protocol is to never approach a celebrity at the studio, which I understand because they are working just like we are.

So there I was, heating my leftovers in the microwave, minding my own business, when I heard him shout out, "Hey . . . whatcha cooking over there?"

I turned around, realizing that he was talking to me. I said, "Leftover Korean food."

"Korean? Kimchi?" he asked.

"No, I'm not a big fan of kimchi." He stood up, extended his hand, and introduced himself.

"Hi, I'm Robert."

Of course I knew who he was! But you gotta play it cool. I responded to him, "Really? My name is Robert too!" and shook his hand.

He laughed and said, "I'll remember that." He then went into this big discussion with me about Korean food and where to get the best kimchi in LA. Pretty hilarious!

When my food was ready, I wished him and his friend a great day and he wished me the same. I told him I had really enjoyed our kimchi conversation, then left the kitchen. I had hoped he would be as cool as I had imagined him to be, and he didn't disappoint. He very much exceeded my expectations.

I even met Harrison Ford when he came in to do some voice-over work for the last *Star Wars* movie he was in. We ran into each other in the hallway. I smiled and said hello and he said, "Where's the commissary? I'm hungry!" I directed him to the kitchen down the hall. He sounded a little bit "hangry." But it's understandable. Han Solo's got to eat! It was exciting to meet him anyway.

I have met several other celebrities over the years, including Jim Carrey, Martin Landau, Amy Poehler, Ryan O'Neal, Zooey Deschanel, Verne Troyer (who played Mini-Me in the *Austin Powers* movies), and even sports legends like Wayne Gretzky and Luc Robitaille back when I worked in radio. I have been fortunate enough to have met a lot of celebrities, and I am happy to say that most of them were really great people. There were some celebrities who unfortunately weren't so nice, which is why they didn't make the cut to be in my book.

I had a preconceived opinion or judgment about each celebrity. What you hear, read, or see on TV isn't necessarily an accurate portrayal of who a person really is. The media is going to go for sensationalism over truth all the time. The question you need to ask yourself is: Where are you getting your information? Is it fact or unsubstantiated gossip?

Using celebrities as an example is easy because there is always a ton of gossip floating around. It's the perfect example to demonstrate where not to get your information. This applies to every person you meet or work with, and even to family. Gossip has no place in formulating valid judgments or opinions. Do your research. Talk to people and get to know them or at least understand them before you start formulating opinions about them. It's easy to jump on the negativity and hate bandwagon, but that is the most toxic thing you can do, not only to others, but to yourself.

The *Dragnet* quote is simple and to the point. Sergeant Friday had it 100% correct when he said, "Just the facts, ma'am." Let that be your mantra when formulating opinions about other people.

TWELVE

Be Patient . . . The Bad Ones Don't Last

Peter Gibbons: "And here's something else, Bob: I have eight different bosses right now."

Bob Slydell: "I beg your pardon?"

Peter Gibbons: "Eight bosses."

Bob Slydell: "Eight?"

Peter Gibbons: "Eight, Bob. So that means that when I make a mistake, I have eight different people coming by to tell me about it. That's my only real motivation is not to be hassled."

Office Space

There are many times when being "micro" is a good thing. For example, probiotics stimulate the growth of microorganisms that are beneficial to your health. Cell phones are another example of "micro," as they are small but powerful computers that fit in the palm of your hand. And for all you beer drinkers, microbreweries are great. In fact, I worked with someone at Disney who left the company to become a microbrewer.

However, there is a "micro" that is a detriment to any workplace: the dreaded micromanager. They exist everywhere, and almost every person I know has had to experience one at some point in their career. The micromanager is such a big problem in the workplace that both *Inc.* and *Forbes* rated bad bosses as the number one reason for work dissatisfaction, and, within that category, micromanagers were ranked at the top of the list.

At this point in my career, I was very adept at working in the encoding department. The file-based world was flourishing, and digital encoding had become the norm. Every project manager was trained in handling encoding work. However, the department was going through revolving door syndrome with managers and supervisors. They couldn't get one to stick. Some were better than others, but none of them lasted.

Since upper management was having a hard time finding a supervisor, they decided to promote from within. One of my coworkers was awarded the honors. She was really excited at the promotion and was champing at the bit to get this opportunity. She said she had a lot of great ideas for the department and was excited to implement them. We were supportive and were ready to see what she had planned.

What started off as exciting soon turned into something we didn't expect. Meetings turned into disciplinary sessions on how we were not doing our jobs correctly. Protocols and SOPs became so complicated it was bogging the department down. Our new supervisor had to be CC'd on every email and would then tell us how we could have sent better messages and how we hadn't followed protocol because we hadn't expressed ourselves in the way she would have communicated. Let the micromanaging games begin!

She micromanaged us so intensely that our hands were tied and we couldn't do our jobs. She somehow acquired access to spreadsheets and sensitive data from other departments in the company, which she should not have had access to. She would go to other departments on the studio lot outside of ours and tell them how they were not doing their jobs efficiently and how she wanted them to do things her way. Needless to say, that did not go over very well, especially since she was usurping another manager's authority from a department she had no business being in. This created more tension, not only within our department, but between departments. Not a good scene. Honestly, I don't know if she was getting pressure from upper management to perform better. Maybe that was pushing her to do what she was doing. Whatever the case, her methods were not working, and her supervision became intolerable.

When it comes to taking on projects and seeing them through, I like to take the bull by the horns, dive right in, and get my projects completed. If there are any issues, I jump right in and do whatever it takes to resolve them. For example, we had a situation with one of the features we were encoding. It was an important project, and a lot of eyes were on it. The problem needed to be solved ASAP. I figured out a way to fix the problem quickly. The client was thrilled with how fast I was able to resolve it. He sent out an email and copied everyone involved to thank me for resolving the issue, and he thanked our department as well. It felt great to be acknowledged and appreciated, especially by this high-profile client. Well, that was short-lived. My supervisor pulled me aside and told me that, although I had solved the client's problem, she could have resolved it better and I should have solved it her way. She reprimanded me for not talking to her about it first, even though she knew what the time constraints had been.

As much as it was torture to work under her supervision, I stuck it out because I knew that she wouldn't last. I wasn't going to let her run me out of my job (some people did quit, though). It took a few months, but the day came when she decided to quit and go work for some other company. That was a victorious day. Patience was a virtue. I had waited it out, and the source of my department's stress and toxic work environment disappeared.

Office Space is such a great movie because it is so relatable. There are many great quotes from that movie, but I picked that particular quote to open the chapter because it represents how a lot of people approach their jobs: just do the bare minimum so they don't get fired. The sad part about it is many people actually love their jobs, but bad management creates toxic work environments, which causes people to hate their jobs. The fact is that, in many cases, it's the environment they hate, not the job itself. Most of the time, it does get better, but you have to be patient.

As intense as my job could be, I enjoyed the work I did. Here are three tips to help you navigate a toxic work environment. The first tip is to stay neutral in negative situations. This will avoid additional conflict and not add fuel to the fire. Second, control what you can, not what you can't. Are you proactive or reactive? Don't allow yourself to be pulled into the drama. You may not be able to control other people, but you can control how you react. Finally, set mental boundaries. Do not let negative actions derail your self-worth. If you need to step away, do it. Take a break and go outside. Change your environment. Get refocused and re-grounded, then go back to your desk.

There are situations where leaving your job is the best option. Use that as a last resort because the grass isn't always greener on the other side. If you like the work that you do, exhaust all possibilities to keep your current job before you decide to move on. See if there is someone you can talk to about any issues. Just make sure you are not one of those people who runs to HR every time they get their feathers ruffled. Be smart about it. If you find your current job is intolerable and the environment will not change, then find a better job, but make sure to do your research before you make a move.

Patience is a virtue and a great tool. I can't tell you how many times I wasn't patient and then regretted my rushed decisions later on. So, exhaust your options and avoid knee-jerk reactions, and you'll see how being patient will get you the best results.

THIRTEEN

That Cup o' Joe Is a No-Go

Red: "I don't know; every man has his breaking point."

The Shawshank Redemption

I wasn't always a coffee drinker. I loved the smell of freshly brewed coffee, but it took me a while to acquire a taste for it. I remember when my coffee addiction began, and it was the Simpsons' fault.

When *The Simpsons Movie* came out, Fox's marketing department converted a couple of 7-Elevens into Kwik-E-Marts. It was a brilliant marketing campaign to promote the movie. I drove from Burbank to the Fox studio lot each morning and passed a Kwik-E-Mart on the way to work. I had no choice but to stop in and grab a coffee. Sometimes I would buy a Homer Simpson donut. This quickly became a morning ritual. Even though I considered 7-Eleven coffee "rocket fuel," the addiction had already rooted itself. If it wasn't for *The Simpsons Movie* and that damn marketing campaign, I would be drinking kombucha instead.

Coffee in the morning is now a daily routine. I love a nice high-quality French roast. Sometimes I'm in the mood for "diner's coffee," but that still has to have flavor to it and not be watered down. I love my cup o' joe!

Now, imagine that cup o' joe isn't coffee but stress. Every day, the "stress cup" fills up, and unless you either get a bigger cup or pour it out, all that stress will overflow. Throughout the book, almost every story I have shared has had an element of stress attached to it. The entertainment industry is notoriously stressful because deadline windows continuously become smaller and smaller. The world is accustomed to immediate gratification, so the pressures of delivering product "yesterday" are the norm.

Before I dive into how to manage the stress cup, I want to clarify that there are two basic forms of stress: good stress and bad stress. Good stress, or "eustress," is a form of stress that is beneficial for performance or health. It energizes and motivates. Examples of eustress might include the butter-flies you get before a performance or a speech or the excite-ment you feel on your wedding day, or the rush that consumes your body when you ride a roller coaster.

On the other hand, bad stress, or "distress," has a negative impact physically and mentally. Distress can cause anxiety, depression, loneliness, loss of appetite, or, on the other hand, binge eating. From a psychological standpoint, it can cause low self-esteem, lack of confidence, lack of self-worth, and even a desire to give up. Sources of distress might include relationship breakups, not meeting a deadline, toxic work environments, and worrying about things that have not come to pass.

There are two methods to manage your stress cup. One is to make a bigger cup, and the other is to empty it out. Doing a combination of both is preferable, but either works fine on its own. Personally, I make the effort to combine both methods.

Let's talk about the first method, creating or building a bigger cup. You need to continuously make your stress cup stronger. Think of it like working out. You are building a bigger and stronger stress cup muscle so you can carry or handle a larger amount of stress *without* taking a toll on your physical and mental health. Some great techniques include meditating, eating healthier, getting enough rest, working out, or doing yoga. Another option is cold therapy or a cold plunge. A cold plunge is basically sitting in a tub of freezing water for three minutes. I have a love–hate relationship with this because of my aversion to cold, but the benefits are well worth it. It boosts your immune system, helps reduce inflammation and arthritis, improves your circulation, and helps boost your metabolism, which aids in weight loss. One of the greatest benefits of doing a cold plunge is that it triggers the production of norepinephrine, which is a neurotransmitter. This chemical helps the body regulate your mental focus and, most importantly, energy. To get the full benefits, you would need to do this on a consistent basis. I do it daily. Honestly, as much as I dread cold plunges, I absolutely feel the benefits.

Ahhh . . . the benefits of a cold plunge.

The second method is emptying the stress cup. When you feel your stress cup filling up to the point of overflowing, you need to empty it right away. Meditation is good for this as well. Breathwork is another great technique that helps balance between the sympathetic and parasympathetic nervous systems, which reduces or empties the stress cup. Immediately stepping away from the environment causing your stress cup to fill is essential. Digital detoxing helps reduce overstimulation in the brain and will empty the cup. Stay away from electronics. Don't grab your phone immediately when you wake up, and put it down at least forty-five minutes before you go to sleep.

Keep in mind that your stress cup may fill up again throughout the day. As long as you are consciously aware of it, you can implement any of the above techniques necessary to empty the stress cup or work the muscle to make it bigger and more resilient. Through consistency, you will develop a habit that will become second nature, and regulating your stress cup will be automatic.

Again, it is imperative to be consciously aware of your stress cup. When you fail to manage your stress and it overflows, that could lead to fight, flight, or freeze, which I talked about in Chapter 9. That was a situation where I did not regulate my stress and it took its toll on me both physically and mentally. If you get to a point where your stress cup overflows, immediately use the techniques I mentioned to stop the overflow and empty the cup.

As I look back on the progression of my career, each step moved me forward. The process that allowed me to continue this forward momentum was managing my stress cup. Even when it seemed like I was being thrown back in the opposite direction, doing a combination of building my stress cup muscle and emptying the cup when it filled kept me motivated to persevere. It also opened my eyes to see how much the events that I experienced played into the overall advancement of my career. For example, being let go from Playboy was a huge blessing. I went back to school to study audio post production, which led to working at a couple of post houses, which eventually led to my job at Fox.

The Shawshank Redemption is one of my favorite movies. Whenever it's on television, no matter what part of the movie I catch, I end up watching it until the end. The quote opening this chapter is said by Morgan Freeman's character, Red. "Every man has his breaking point." In other words, every person can handle only so much stress before the cup overflows. I had the chance to meet Frank Darabont, the director of *Shawshank*, when I worked on the film *The Majestic* with Jim Carrey. Darabont had such a level-headed demeanor but still ran a tight ship. Not only did he know how to manage his own stress cup, his approach to directing kept his actors and crew from stressing out during the production, which helped manage their stress cups as well.

Another quote I considered using was from *Bruce Almighty*. Jim Carrey's character, Bruce, is doing a human interest story that's being broadcast live, and he hears in his earpiece that Evan Baxter, his archnemesis, got the news anchor job he wanted. Bruce's stress cup overflows like a dam breaking. As he is interviewing an old woman, his anger gets the best of him and he loses it. Making fun of her and comparing her to Rose from the movie *Titanic*, he blurts out, "Did you feel bad at all letting Leo DiCaprio drown while you were safe floating on that big door?!" It's a funny scene, as only Jim Carrey can make it, but it demonstrates what happens when you allow your stress cup to overflow. However, I felt the quote from *The Shawshank Redemption* was more appropriate.

I created a list of six techniques to reduce stress. It's a great reference tool that will help you manage your stress cup. Grab this and all the other free bonuses that go with the book at the link— bit.ly/3L02Z7Q-FreeBonuses —or scan the QR code at the end of the chapter.

How about we switch from the stress cup to a plain ol' mug and fill it with the elixir of life, a nice big cup o' joe? It's much more tasty!

That Cup o' Joe Is a No-Go

Free Bonuses!

FOURTEEN

And I–Eee–I . . . Will Always Love Me

Elizabeth: "We don't have to be afraid anymore."

Drop Dead Fred

I love me. I love me not. I love me. I love me not. Yes, it's that old game of picking petals off a flower to see if you are loved or not, but with a twist. It's exciting when the person you are attracted to reciprocates your love, but are you just as excited about the love you have for yourself?

After wanting to be a stuntman, my next dream job was to be a rock star. When I was thirteen, I found a beat-up old acoustic guitar in the hall closet. My dad said his dad had given it to him, but neither ever learned to play. We took the guitar to a local music store to get it fixed up, and *voilà*, I was on my way to rock stardom! The first song I taught myself how to play was "Day Tripper" by The Beatles. I started writing my own songs not too long after. I called this my "Campfire Tunes" phase. The songs were pretty bad and really goofy, but a rock star has to start somewhere.

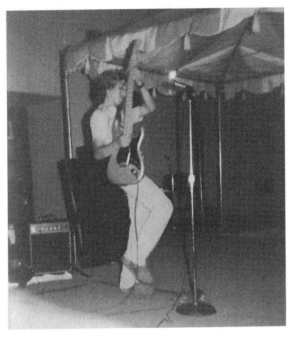

My first band—rock star in training . . .

I eventually put a band together with friends from school. I was supposed to be the lead singer as well as the guitarist, but my lack of confidence and belief in my own voice made me decide not to take on the lead singer responsibility. Even when my bandmates told me to sing, I said no and told one of the other guys to do it. To this day, I regret that decision because I stopped myself from doing something that I loved and wanted to do. Did I have a great voice? Well, I don't think I'd pass the audition for *America's Got Talent*, but I wasn't dreadful. Because I allowed my fears and low self-esteem to get the best of me, it took longer than it should have for me to get over this false belief.

When I was in eleventh grade, I started writing poetry because it was one of our assignments in honors English class. This actually inspired me to continue writing, and I eventually wrote three poetry books. Much of it was based on my life experiences at that time. Going through life post-high school and throughout my twenties was definitely a period of self-discovery. The books themselves were called *The Dark Side Vol. I*, *The Dark Side Vol. III*, and *Love Poems, For A Change*. The third book, *Love Poems, For A Change*, had good intentions at first, but it ended up being just as dark as the other two books. It included a poem I had written called "Not Good Enough," which basically admitted that I had not accomplished anything of substance or real significance in my life. The poem reflected a limiting belief that I was not and never would be good enough. Even though the books were completed, I never published them. I felt that they were not good enough.

The lack of self-love can stem from a culmination of other issues, including low self-worth, low self-esteem, and low confidence. Although these are contributors to not loving yourself, it is important to understand the basic differences between them so that you don't confuse them for or define them as self-love.

Self-love is embracing your entire self, all of your abilities, and all of your failings. You accept who you are completely. You are kind and caring and 100% committed to yourself. Signs of lacking self-love include feeling that you are not lovable so you look outside of yourself to find someone or something to fill the void. People who lack self-love tend to be needy or have chaotic relationships. Some wear masks to hide their vulnerability.

Self-worth is the opinion and the value you place upon yourself. This can contribute to your self-love in a positive or negative way. Feeling worthy allows you to embrace your entire self. Feeling worthless does the opposite.

Self-esteem is how you think and feel about yourself based on internal or external influences. It is a set of beliefs you carry with you, whether they are true or not. Self-esteem can be based on mood, experience, or achievements.

Finally, confidence is trusting and believing that you are capable of accomplishing any task, no matter how difficult. Confidence does not allow self-doubt to enter the picture. You believe in your intellect, your interaction with others, and your ability to be successful.

Again, all of the above can be contributors to self-love, either in a positive or a negative way. When you don't love yourself, you create barriers or roadblocks that keep you from moving forward with your life. I coached a few clients who had self-love issues that were rooted in situations that had occurred when they were children. We were able to strip away the layers and get down to the root causes. Eventually, they were able to break down the barriers that were keeping them from loving themselves. Once the barriers were gone, there was nothing to stop them from attaining true self-love.

Do you love yourself? Do you love who you see in the mirror? This goes beyond what you physically see. Do you love the person that you are? If the answer to any of these questions is no, you need to ask yourself why. Make sure you are brutally honest when you unravel the "why." If you are not being honest with yourself, who do you think you are fooling?

I'd like to share one more story with you. It's about self-sabotage, something so many people are guilty of. Back in college, a really good friend of mine was taking courses and also had a job to help pay for school. Even though her employer was aware that she was a college student, her boss would keep asking her to work more hours, and it was cutting into her class time. I told her to tell her boss that she had classes and remind him that he knew she was a student, but she decided to work instead. This happened more and more until she eventually had to drop all of her classes. She was upset and said, "You see, everything happens to me." I told her that she had set herself up for failure because she didn't set boundaries with her job. I asked why she had done that to herself, but she didn't have an answer. It boiled down to her not loving and believing in herself. She didn't think she had the ability to do well in her classes. She was afraid to step out of her comfort zone and wanted to avoid failure at all costs. She had a negative and demeaning perspective about herself and her life. But by trying to avoid failure at all costs, she ended up setting herself up for failure after all.

To garner any level of success in life, you have to love yourself. You have to embrace the incredibly awesome person that you are and believe it. Truly loving yourself is hard, especially in the world we live in. You are constantly bombarded with external forces that influence your perception of yourself. You have been groomed to think and feel a certain way. Some of the perceptions stem from childhood. Other factors are the messy habits or even the baggage your parents brought into your home life. Then there are the demands and expectations of the world and society as a whole. Social media has a huge effect by presenting fake and overblown expectations of how you should look and act. You are always trying to fit a mold, and your true self gets lost in the shuffle. You're too fat, too skinny, too assertive, too shy, too loud, too quiet. You lose sight of your core beliefs and become completely sidetracked from the person you really are.

Here are a few things to keep in mind that can help you build self-love. First, it's okay to not be okay. This phrase is becoming more popular, and for good reason. Accepting that things are not perfect and working through fears that stop you from loving yourself will help you get through any challenges that come up. Be okay with discomfort and don't make things bigger than they really are. Know that no matter what the challenge is, you will be okay.

Ditch perfectionism. Your perception of perfectionism may not be perfect at all. In other words, what feels perfect for you may not be perfect for someone else. All this means is that there are aspects of perfectionism that are subjective. Make sure what you consider "perfect" is actually what you want, not based on what someone else believes. If striving for perfectionism is holding you back from loving yourself, ditch it!

You must be able to forgive yourself. I have seen many people opening their hearts to forgive others but, when it comes to themselves, slamming the door shut. Again, no one is perfect. To truly love others, you must love and forgive yourself. These phrases may sound cliché and may be overused at times, but there is truth in those words. Cut yourself some slack and open yourself to self-forgiveness.

Along with forgiving yourself is allowing yourself to make mistakes. Yes, that means you are not perfect, so you know what to do: ditch perfectionism! See how all of this is tied together? Along with making mistakes is having the integrity to own up to them. When you truly love yourself, you have no problem being accountable and honorable enough to admit mistakes and apologize, if necessary. Mistakes are part of the human process of life.

Thank your body. Thank this physical being that sustains you. Be grateful that you woke up in the morning and that you can breathe and walk and feel and see and hear. You may have ailments, and there could be parts of your body that don't work as well as you'd like them to, but thank your body for what you have. Respecting and appreciating your physical body is a means to expressing self-love.

You are a wonderful, empowered being that deserves love. You need to tell yourself that you love *you*! Before you go to bed, stand in front of the mirror. Look yourself straight in the eye, say your name, and tell yourself one or two affirmations (or as many as you want). "I am awesome!" "I am proud of myself!" Take a deep breath, look deep into your eyes, and say, "I love you." Repeat those words until you genuinely feel them. It may take one minute or twenty minutes, but keep saying "I love you" until you feel it in your core. Finally, take it all in with a big deep breath in through the nose and out through the mouth. You are pulling this into your subconscious. Remember, your beliefs and habits are the fuel that drives your subconscious and affects your daily decisions.

Make this practice a new habit you do every night. This will become second nature and a permanent routine. In fact, this new habit should be a nonnegotiable for the rest of your life. You are good enough. You are loved. You are love.

As you grow more genuine love for yourself, it will allow you to define your life purpose. Life purpose isn't just a goal. It is a means by which you live your life as a way of being, rather than doing. Visualize what your life would be like when you do the things that matter to you. For example, a life purpose statement could be something like "My life purpose is to support people in using their gifts and making their dreams come true."

Another way of looking at your life purpose is to think of it as your personal mission statement. Almost every business, no matter how big or small, has a mission statement. I find that over 98% of my clients have never created any personal mission statement, let alone thought about their life purpose. Everyone should create a personal mission statement. Start with writing down your core beliefs and values. What beliefs, morals, and priorities make you who you are? Then take a global look at ways you can make a difference in the world. Scale down your view from global to community to family and write them down. Next, write down your goals—and be specific. Are they aligned with your core beliefs and values? Finally, think about some of your past accomplishments. Are there any common themes? Who did those accomplishments benefit? Gather up all this information and create your personal mission statement.

In addition to having a personal mission statement, you need to have a support system. It could be a spouse, friend, or family member or a coach. Surround yourself with positive people. Surround yourself with people who can do things better than you can because that will push you toward greatness faster. Keep in mind that misery loves company and will seek you out, but there is no room for any form of misery in your life. Finally, make the most out of the life that you have been given. When you truly love yourself, you will easily enjoy the life you have, and you will also be motivated to make it even better.

Drop Dead Fred is such a fun and zany movie, but it has some great life lessons. The quote is said towards the end of the movie, where adult Elizabeth is rescuing herself, little Elizabeth. The scene plays out where little Elizabeth is bound to her bed with masking tape, and adult Elizabeth frees her. This is a very poignant scene, as adult Elizabeth has broken the proverbial chains that have kept her trapped most of her life. She now can love herself again. As she hugs little Elizabeth and tells her, "We don't have to be afraid anymore," she embraces her fears, works through them, and then lets them go. Those fears had crushed her confidence, self-esteem, and self-love throughout her life. Now that she has come to terms with them, her confidence and self-love immediately skyrocket.

You must genuinely love yourself before you can love others. Self-love is not easy because people confuse it with being selfish. Self-love is self-respect. Self-love is making your mental and physical health a priority. I know many people who bend over backward to help others but put their own self-care on the back burner—or worse, don't practice self-care at all. Take care of yourself. Love yourself. This is something you can't fake. You are more transparent than you think. Helping others can be part of your personal mission statement, but always make self-love and self-care your number one priorities.

So Now What?

Many people get fired up to make positive changes to their lives but don't follow through because they don't have a support system or someone to guide them through their journey. I want you to take decisive action to master your mindset, overcome work stress, and regain your personal freedom.

If you are struggling with any of the issues I discussed in the book, whether at your job or in your personal life, reach out to me. Many career professionals who have gone through my coaching program, The Mindset Method, were able to transform their lives permanently. They were able to love their jobs again, get promoted faster, or land their next-level roles with more pay, meaning, and purpose. Also, they attained more personal freedom to enjoy their lives on their terms.

Remember, to achieve the awesome life you deserve, there's only one simple step: *take decisive action*. Here are a few easy ways to get in touch with me to learn more about The Mindset Method program and how to enroll:

Website: https://www.robertlanecoaching.com/

Email: support@rrpproducts.com

Instagram: @robertlanecoaching

You can also set up a quick fifteen-minute assessment call with me so we can discuss what your struggles are, where you want to be, and how I can help you reach your goals. I'll also go over how you can enroll in The Mindset Method program. Click below to schedule your call:

Robert Lane Coaching Assessment Call (https://calendly.com/robertlanecoaching/assessment)

Or scan the code below:

Acknowledgments

Jason Risk, Jake Kelfer, Mahwish Syed, Telma Sanchez, Lisa Marie Doxey, Darneatha Lawrence, Gerald Lane, Irene Lane, Sheila Swann, Robert A. Mattey, Craig Mattey, Fox Studios, Felicia Kaplan, Jacques Pintone, Brian May, Robert Downey Jr., Juli Ashton, Jeana Taylor, Fox Media Services, Weird Al Yankovic, Tom Cruise, George Clooney, Tiffany Granath, Brenda Jack, Gigi Santoro, Frank Crim, Tabatha Jones, Gina Delgado, Elizabeth Lopez, Jose Lopez, Batgirl Escobedo, Bethany Davis, Tam Tran, Gay Acosta Newlin, Rebecca Babcock, Steve Walsh, Jeff Levicke, Nettie Lu Lane, Aubri Lane, Selene Chavarria, Claire Smedley, Elier Lopez, CRN Networks, Post Logic Studios, Helen F. Sullivan, Aaron Gould, Missy Handy, Ed Gillow, Marlene Kuo-Morinaga, Cynthia Yokoyama, Liza Crawford-Vondriska, Zander Fryer, Shane Youngerman, Deb Lauren, Wayne Gretzky, Ed Gillow, Kennedy Waite, Bruce Buehlman, Brian Pierson, Bryan Downey, John Gullett, Gabby Arriaza, Alisha Burr, Rick Obradors, Chris Gardner, Erik Wiggins, Jr., Maureen Wiggins, Keith Sam, Jennifer Horn, Michael Horn, Eric Chase, Rob Collins, Jackie Peretti, Robert Grimm, Burke Greer, Grace Garcia, Wes Cook, Diana Bauder, Gabe Bernard, LC Calverley, Robert Papp, Andrew Chung, T. Arthur Cottam, Kiff Scholl, Grace Hong, Adam Princenthal, Kelly Van Valkenburg, Megan Togno

Special thanks to Aileen Hitomi Lane for all her love and support.

About the Author

Robert A. Lane is a corporate performance coach, dynamic motivational speaker, and stress management facilitator. He works with enterprising career professionals, helping them achieve true work-life balance and personal freedom by eliminating stress, overwhelm, and burnout.

In *Lights, Action, YOU!*, Robert uses his thirty-plus years of experience working in various facets of the entertainment industry to exemplify the tools and techniques he teaches in his coaching program The Mindset Method, which has helped many people achieve stress-free lives permanently.

Robert works with his clients in both one-on-one and group sessions. He also does workshops, presentations and lunch-and-learns for businesses and corporations all over the United States.

Robert is also an award-winning filmmaker and an accomplished film composer. He resides in Sedona, Arizona.

Connect with Robert at www.robertlanecoaching.com or on social at @robertlanecoaching!

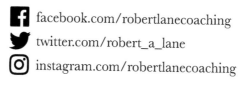

facebook.com/robertlanecoaching

twitter.com/robert_a_lane

instagram.com/robertlanecoaching

Spread the Word!

I just want to say a quick thank you for reading the book and that I am truly grateful. I hope you enjoyed the stories but, most importantly, learned some valuable life lessons from my experiences in the entertainment industry. The techniques in the book apply to any career in any industry, and they can also be applied to your personal life.

If the book resonated with you, please talk about it to your friends, family and social media. I would also love it if you left a review on Amazon - https://amzn.to/3xxncfA. Your support is greatly appreciated!

Lights, Action, YOU!
Scan code to write a
review on Amazon!